BRO-KIN BRANCH

by

James Robert Dowell

authorHOUSE®

AuthorHouse™
1663 Liberty Drive, Suite 200
Bloomington, IN 47403
www.authorhouse.com
Phone: 1-800-839-8640

First published by AuthorHouse   4/21/2008

ISBN: 978-1-4343-5035-0 (sc)
ISBN: 978-1-4343-5036-7 (hc)

Printed in the United States of America
Bloomington, Indiana

This book is printed on acid-free paper.

Acknowledgments

I want to thank my dear wife, Jane, for all the hard work she has contributed to this book, for which I am deeply grateful. We share the same enthusiasm and interest in our genealogy and ancestry. Her constant encouragement and enthusiasm for this uniquely human subject is truly amazing.

Because of the skillful and professional assistance rendered by my friend, Keith Warn, this is a better book. Thank you.

The minds and hearts of many people have gone into this book, for which I deeply appreciate. Sharing their lives has reinforced my belief that we all share the same goals, loves and aspirations.

ACKNOWLEDGMENTS

CONTENTS

"DEVOTIONAL"

I felt compelled to add a devotional to my story of ancestral discovery and connection. I'm not claiming to have been a devout spiritual person for most of my life, Lord knows I've had my sinful way. But, I feel it's important to reveal that if it weren't for the Lord, redirecting my life, I wouldn't have written this book. This is partly due to my life being mostly about me and my success and self-gratification. It never brought me the satisfaction I expected.

The new direction I've discovered has left me seeking others to share my exuberance about life with. Out of this new direction has come a desire to know more about my past, my ancestry. Did they have some of the same feelings I felt? Did they have some of the same experiences?

I felt honored and exceedingly grateful to discover that my ancestors brought the Lord with them upon coming to America. They brought Him in their hearts, their minds and in their bibles. They built churches in his name and preached, taught, and lived the word of the Lord. Many of the Commandments were at the root of their pioneering spirit, which was revealed in the compassion, concern, and service they rendered to those in need. As a righteous community they laughed together, cried together and prayed together and shared the love of the Lord.

Fig. 1　Author, James Robert Dowell, Standing Near His
　　　　Birthplace of Carlsbad, New Mexico

FOREWORD

The amazing history of the Dowell's journey from the old country to America is truly astonishing. Their story covers several generations of pioneering efforts. The times were hard and full of peril as they landed in Virginia, eventually moving West.

This is their story, of pain, struggle and moments of glory as they ventured to new territory and settled in their new found land. The underlying thread that runs through their history, is a strong faith in our Lord. They brought Him with them as they journeyed, in their hearts and souls and in their Bible. With their pioneering spirit, came an ambition to make a new life for themselves. They helped tame the wild West and forged a new way of life. The life they chose was to fulfill their destiny, where freedom loving people could have a chance to live in peace and prosperity.

As they moved West, their stories of sacrifice, heroism and prosperity began to unfold. They were caught up in the whirlwind of history, as America proclaimed its freedom in the Revolutionary War. Then the war with Mexico began its epic cry for expansion further West. Fate, however, would have no part of any eternal peace and along came the Civil War. It was a time of choosing sides and fighting for one's beliefs. The results were devastating, as brother fought against brother. The pain and suffering inflicted on both sides, was beyond what anyone could ever imagine. The land of our country turned red with the blood of thousands upon thousands of Americans fighting for their cause. As quickly as it began, they awoke to a new day of peace and tranquility. The Union remained in-tact with the South acquiescing to its demands to free the slaves and "One Country Under God." As our country picked up the pieces of a new way of life, it began to grow again with the discovery of gold in California.

The call went out far and wide across the country; "California or Bust". The new settlers came by the thousands seeking their fortune in a hostile land, full of danger and lack of law and order. Nevertheless, the desire for a new life beckoned its call as the pioneers battled the Indian tribes for their land. The prairie was full of old broken furniture and dreams strewn across its trails to the West, as pain and suffering welcomed the weary travelers. This was not what they expected, but they knew that anything worth while had its dues. The age of prosperity once again returned to America, as fortunes were made and lost at the drop of a hat. There were more wars to be fought for sure but for now, it was time to grow and become the mightiest country the world had ever known. Who would have thought at that time that America would be called to preserve the peace of the world on many occasions in its future.

As our country paid in blood for its existence and love of freedom, many battles have been fought and won. The brave men and women of the Dowell family and their relatives answered the call of World War I and then World War II, with the same pioneering spirit that drew them to America and the West. The quest for peace soon alluded us again, as America fought the Korean War, Vietnam War and is now embroiled in the second Iraq conflict. What price peace, remains our cry. When will the quests of our foreign neighbors to plunder and bring death to their innocent, stop? You can be sure that our proud and freedom loving country will stand by those around the world seeking what we have. As Americans, we have all paid the price in one way or another. The brave, the proud, the men and women who protect our country from those who would seek to destroy it, remain strong and willing to defend it to the end. This is what their sons and daughters were called to do as well as our sons and daughters, as we endeavor to give privilege to the lost, the poor, and the deprived around the world. The same pioneering spirit that made this country what it is. The love of God, Country and freedom, will endure. We can be proud of our ancestors as they displayed the strength, determination, character and compassion for what is good and true. We are what they represented. . . . after all, they are our family.

Many people fail to see the value of looking back to their ancestral roots. Their feelings are usually exemplified by statements like; "they lived their times, now it's our turn to live ours!: The interesting thing to note about a study of family history, is the knowledge of why we act and feel the way we do about life in general. The acts of kindness and compassion towards our fellowman were underscored and handed down from generation to generation. What we are, what we learned and lived from a young age, we owe to our parents. They in turn learned from their parents. This is God's intended way, as he created marriage, parents and family. The love of God and Country, as well as family roots, has made this country the most talked about, the most revered and loved country the world has ever known.

As families grew and prospered, it was not uncommon to hear parents say to their son, "you remind me so much of your grandfather so and so" , or to a daughter, "you look and act just like your Aunt so and so!" These connections are not just happen-chance, they are handed down. Just like our physical looks, so do we inherit personality traits like emotion and mannerisms. I believe that "to look back, is to look ahead!"

Our future lies in our past. The character, the strengths and determination portrayed and lived by our ancestors is what will allow us to succeed in the future. We know what we are made of, as witnessed and exemplified by our illustrious ancestry. We have seen them time and time again, answer the call to duty. By their willingness and heroic acts to protect our country and fight for freedom around the world, they have shown us the way. Their compassion and sacrifice for others, fills history books, that bring us honor and glory throughout the world.

In writing this book of my ancestry, I was moved by the character they portrayed. There were laughable moments and tearful times as I attempted to reach out to them over the ages. I found myself struggling with them emotionally as they suffered and persevered. I also found comfort and joy in their happiest times. This was truly a journey of love and compassion for what they stood for and lived throughout their lives. For that I am deeply grateful. Through my efforts in searching and revealing my ancestral history, the knowledge I grew up and lived without, will be available to future generations through this book. There will be no doubt that they do, in fact, have a family history.

Chapter I

Forsaken Heritage

As a child I grew up knowing nothing about my dad's relatives. Surprisingly neither did my brothers and sisters. It was a well kept secret simply because my father refused to discuss his past. This left our family to wonder and fabricate stories that may or may not be true. What happened to make my father feel the way he did about his past? Did his breaking of family ties have anything to do with the fact that his father, Elijah Dowell was in prison for who knows what? Could his father's family have disowned him for shame he may have brought their family? This lack of information other than my dad's father being incarcerated for five years in Huntsville Penitentiary, left us to wonder why.

There were stories about my father being adopted and brought up by a neighbor family. There was a story that he was an only child from an illegitimate marriage. The last of any information left our family in the dark about his father's true past. Whatever left my dad so estranged from his family's past may never fully be known. He was never willing to discuss his childhood or teenage years. If he was pushed for any information, he would just reply with a sarcastic remark like, "why do you need to know?" or "it doesn't matter, so just forget it!"

My mother's family was just the opposite. She was one of sixteen children, so we had many Uncles, Aunts, and Cousins on her side of the family. She told many stories of her past, and her ancestry. She related how her older brothers and sisters were born in Mexico, before her family crossed the Rio Grande River into El Paso, Texas, during the late 1800's. One story she told was about an incident that occurred when she was a child. She remembered living in a small cabin in the woods with many brothers and sisters. On one particular day, she recalled that her father left the cabin to go to town for needed supplies. Later that evening, she was told by her mother that the family had to lie down for the night and remain very quiet. When they asked, their mother stared at them with a frightened look on her face, as she replied, "I saw two Indians climb upon the roof, they are waiting for your father so they can steal his supplies!" The family quietly huddled together in fear as they prayed for their father's safety. During the night, they could hear someone moving around on their cabin roof. They began to pray that their father would not return until after daybreak the following day, as the Indians would leave for fear of being seen in the daylight.

The night was long as they remained huddled together in the dark, watching their mother pace the floor. Just as daylight began to break, they heard the Indians leave the roof top. They anxiously waited for their father to return, knowing he would be safe now that the Indians were gone, and their prayers were answered.

The silence that surrounded my dad's past was honored by all of our family, simply due to his refusal to discuss it. It was as though it never existed. Since my dad didn't care to discuss his past, we just willingly accepted the silence about his kin folk.

On June 11, 1979 our father passed away taking all his family secrets with him.

Our only connection to his past was his father's first name. My mother, who left us a few years later, also remained silent about what little she may or may not have known about his past. As a family, we were led to believe that our ancestry was of no consequence. Many years and questions had gone unanswered and no real evidence of our dad's past surfaced until I was in my late teens.

Many years later as my oldest brother, Bob, and I were discussing our ancestry, he revealed that when he took our dad on a trip to Mexico via El Paso, Texas, they stopped there for a short while. This was sometime in the early seventies and during the time they were there, our dad told him that he had an aunt by the name of Mary Phillips living in El Paso, Texas. When my brother suggested they look her up and give her a phone call, my dad refused to follow up on a search for her. This was the first time my dad revealed that his father, Elijah Dowell, had a sister. Apparently he knew of her and that she was living in El Paso, but refused to look for her.

In the early thirties, when my family lived in Lakewood, New Mexico, my older brothers and sisters recall our Grandpa Elijah (Lige) living near them. As small children, they remember him bringing sacks of vegetables from the local fields for them to eat. He would tell them stories of the old West. Their memories of him were happy and cheerful, as he would tease them and at times bring them toys he would make out of wood he had carved. They remember that their grandmother, his wife, had passed away many years before at an early age, leaving him all alone. This was the extent of their knowledge about our heritage. Elijah Dowell, our grandpa, died in 1937 in Carlsbad, New Mexico, a small town near Lakewood. My family attended the funeral. His death was from natural causes, and it was recorded that his burial took place in Carlsbad, Eddy County, New Mexico.

It was in the early seventies when my curious niece, Delphina decided to visit the City of El Paso, Texas. She had heard that her grandpa, my father, had lived in El Paso and met my mother, her grandmother, there. This is also the place where they married. It was also later revealed by my niece, that my father would tell her stories of his past! These stories were never told to his son's or daughter's, and left us puzzled as to why he failed to mention them. In family discussions about unknown ancestry, my niece related that her grandpa would tell her many stories of his childhood.

These little known stories were of his grandpa, Benjamin Dowell, who was said to have been the first Mayor of El Paso, Texas. The stories went on to include events that left her curious about what she could find out if she went to El Paso. To our families surprise, Delphina had brought back numerous newspaper clippings of who was believed to be our great grandfather. His name was Benjamin Shacklett Dowell and his prominence in El Paso's history was astonishing. He was documented to be the first Mayor of El Paso and owned the first saloon known as the Monte Carlo of the West. Our great grandfather was also said to be a soldier in two wars; the Mexican American War and the Civil War. He was a postmaster, landowner, horseman, sportsman, stock financier, grocery and meat market owner, carpenter, wagon maker, surveyor, Commissioner, County Assessor, and agriculturist. He was El Paso's first scientific farmer, introducing sweet potatoes, alfalfa and tobacco to the area. The record went on to say that he married a Tigua Indian princess and had one daughter and four sons, one of which was Elijah Dowell, my grandfather. The stories and pictures depicted in newspaper clippings were exciting to read. I wrestled with the idea for some time, and came to the erroneous conclusion that this was a non-related Dowell as I had come across Dowell's in the past who were not related. I felt that if they were related, my dad would have surely said something about them, being that they were such a prominent family. Since my father failed to authenticate the news about Benjamin Shacklett Dowell our great grandfather, I gave up on the idea that he was. This was the last time I heard anything about my dad's relatives prior to his death.

There were various stories that circulated over the years that never were proven to be true. Therefore, I never took any information received as a known fact. My father continued to remain silent and refused to talk about his side of the family when questioned about it. What could have turned him against his family, no one knows. He remained adamant about remaining silent and went to his grave with the truth about his past.

As I recall what it was like to live at my parents home when I was a child, I remember my dad's stern, stubborn way he brought us up. He used fear to control us and many times left us puzzled at his over reaction at such trivial things. He seemed to have an inappropriate anger that revealed itself at the slightest agitation. It would, at times, turn into a rage of monstrous proportions especially when he'd been drinking.

The reactions he displayed were obvious to many, that he appeared to be harboring some deep feelings and resentment about some past situations that never were resolved. This resentment he carried, left little or no room for a loving, caring father he could have been. Whatever occurred to break up his family ties, left him with unresolved anger that affected our entire family life.

Chapter II

A Trip to the Past

On a day much like any other, my wife Jane was working on her Creative Memories book. She had looked through all of her family albums and gathered many pictures of her families past. Her interest in her heritage was renewed by our daughter Lisa, who began selling "Creative Memories" products. This renewed interest, resulted in many hours of work on a heritage album. A weekend trip was planned by Lisa and her friends, to a mountain retreat in Big Bear, California, where they would share their interest in Creative Memories keepsake albums and scrapbooks. My wife was invited to go along with her daughter and partake in the scrap booking retreat where she would be able to give and receive ideas with others.

Upon their return, Jane shared her heritage album she had worked on for two days on her trip. I must admit, I was amazed and excited to see what a beautiful job she had done. Her album depicted four generations of pictures and stories relating to her past. I could see the pride she felt in knowing and reliving her ancestral past, as she turned the pages and shared her heritage with me. Since her heritage album was such a success, Jane wanted to include more of her family tree. This led her to join an internet site called Ancestry.com. Once she began her ancestry search, she realized that her album was only a small part of what was later to be discovered. In her words "It was like a revelation of major proportions, as generations of family began to appear all the way back to Europe in the 1700's. In a matter of weeks, her Creative Memories album became a who's who of family heritage pictures and stories. They related a long line of strong pioneers who made their successes through hard work and perseverance.

Like many of the early pioneers, Jane's ancestors were farmers and railroad workers,who helped establish towns and communities. They enjoyed playing music, as many were musicians and spent their leisure hours getting together and playing their favorite songs to the delight of their family members. After seeing all the information that Jane was able to compile from various sources, I was saddened to think that I was without an ancestral past, or so it seemed. My father never spoke much of his heritage, to the extent that our family didn't even know his mother's name! To see Jane's heritage "come alive" so to speak, left me wondering if any search for my past would turn up anything. One day as we were discussing her success at researching her heritage, I asked her if she could find the time to check on my silent past. Jane was willing to seek some Dowell's on her Ancestry program and asked me to give her a few days to check on it. She later admitted that she felt that a few minutes of searching would reveal little and she could get back to work on her side of the family.

A few days later, seemingly out of nowhere, a history that was to astonish and shock us both, began to reveal itself. I felt an emotional high, as Jane printed sheet after sheet of my ancient family history. My heritage was not only real, it was filled with prominent people and stories going back to the Mexican American War and the Civil War. My excitement over the discovery of such a colorful past left me totally amazed at what my father had taken to the grave with him. He could have shared such wonderful stories of bravery, strength, and compassion but chose to remain silent. My only thought was why?

As Jane and I continued to research my side of the family, it was plain to see that we had struck a gold mine of ancient history. The emotions I experienced where similar to finding a long lost friend who had disappeared only to reappear again. I became so engrossed in all the information about my ancestry, that I began to discuss the possibility of a trip to El Paso, Texas where my Great Grandfather Benjamin Shacklett Dowell was the first mayor. The stories of him began to unfold as though it were a movie. It moved me to want to seek more of his illustrious past. As Jane's research took us further and further into my Great Grandfathers life, it gave us the incentive to seek more and more. We began to realize that only a trip to the scene of such great stories would satisfy our hunger. This eventually found us packing and planning a trip to El Paso, Texas where it all began.

Since we were living in Southern California, a trip to Texas was not considered that far away. We couldn't find a small travel trailer to rent so we purchased one, which would allow us to take our prized poodle, Coco, along with us. We gave ourselves a week's time to do the round trip and upon leaving home, we prayed and hoped we could find relatives still living there. We took the route through San Diego and followed the route through Arizona, New Mexico then Texas. This was the same route taken by my Great Grandfather on his way to Los Angeles during the late 1800's. We reached the Texas border no less for wear, and were surprised to see a large tourist center with a sign saying "Welcome to Texas". We concluded that the first thing we were going to need was a phone directory. We could then look up some Dowell's and hopefully meet with them. Our first lesson in looking up lost relatives was, it's not that easy! The only thing we had going for us was determination to succeed. We were going to find family if we had to search all of El Paso.

We decided to check out the downtown library which to our surprise was a huge building housing thousands upon thousands of books and a large section of historical books, records and newspaper clippings. Our luck was about to change, as we realized that the few Dowell's that were in the phone book may have been related, but didn't know it, or simply didn't care, one way or another. We knew my Dad had made a comment to my older brother back in the early 60's, that he had an Aunt named Mary Phillips living in El Paso. The research of records in the library kept leading us to the Phillips families that resided in El Paso. My Great Grandfathers first child, Mary Dowell, had married a Warner Phillips as a young woman. We realized, as strange as it seemed that we were looking for the wrong family. In order to find the lost family we were looking for, we had to search for the Phillips family that a Dowell had become.

We were able to find numerous articles and pictures of the Dowell legacy in El Paso, after all my great grandfather was the first mayor. The first thought we had as we entered the library was that we were going to have to request micro-fiche to get our information. To our surprise, the library staff stated, "we have numerous records on the Dowell history in newspaper clippings and story books." We spent hours going over all the exciting stories and pictures that were laid before us. It was truly an exciting and emotional moment, to see my family heritage come alive.

Once we began to digest all the information, our research still had not yielded any phone numbers or addresses to contact. We went back to our travel trailer, loaded down with numerous copies of pictures and newspaper stories of my Great Grandfathers life in El Paso and marriage to Juana Marquez, a Tigua Indian princess.

As we sifted through the newly found information, the name of Robert Phillips came up as a grandson of Mary Dowell Phillips. I quickly grabbed the phone book and began to look for the name of Robert Phillips. There were many Phillips in the book, but I was almost sure there would be a Phillips that was somehow connected to our family. Bingo! There it was. A Robert Phillips plain as day. I quickly grabbed the phone and began to dial the number. Before I could complete the call, Jane yelled out at me, "what are you doing? Its past nine o'clock and too late to make calls!" I hung up the phone, thinking how close I came to possibly making contact with lost ancestors and current family relatives. I looked up at her and said "I've been waiting for this moment for more than fifty years". She smiled as though she was saying, "O.K.break the rules, the moment calls for it!"

I quickly grabbed the phone and began to dial again. The phone rang and rang and rang. As I was going to hang up, some what disappointed, the call was answered. An old but alert voice answered "hello, this is the Robert Phillips residence." I was nervous and excited as I told him who I was and from where and whom I was seeking.

He replied in a surprised voice, "I'm Robert Phillips and my Grandmother was Mary Dowell Phillips." He went on to give me more history of his family, as I raised my hand up to Jane with a smile on my face; we made contact! I was actually speaking to a relative, somewhat removed from our family tree, but he was the first family member on my Dad's side I had ever spoken to in my entire life. In my excitement, I took his address and directions. Then to my surprise, he invited us to his home that night. We quickly got ready and attempted to find his place, but the streets were dark and the signs were hard to read. In frustration, we called Robert Phillips and postponed our meeting until the following day. I found it difficult to sleep that night, as I kept thinking what our first family reunion of sorts would be like.

The following morning found us up early and getting ready for our visit to Robert. Upon my knock at his door, a small Mexican lady answered, who we found later to be Robert's care taker. She let me in, as Jane chose to wait in the car with our poodle until I called for her. As I entered the small living room, I was told to have a seat and Robert would soon be there. I looked up at the wall and there were three large framed portraits of my Great Grandfather Benjamin Shacklett Dowell, his wife Juana Marquez and his daughter Mary Dowell Phillips. There was no doubt that I had found the right place. As I waited, I could hear someone approaching the living room through a long hallway, sounding as though they were using a walker. I looked up and there he was, a tall man looking his years, but very alert and quick to respond to a hand shake. It was difficult to believe that he was ninety five years old and appeared in good health. I quickly called my wife in from the car, and our first family reunion began.

We felt right at home as we talked about how we were related and what we went through to find him. Later we were joined by Roberts daughter, Mary Jane. She was as friendly as her father, and made our visit a memorable one. We soon learned that Robert had two daughters; Mary Jane who lived nearby and Patty who lived near Houston, Texas.

Robert's wife Celia passed away in 2004. Robert's sister, Chella, and his wife Celia were professional tennis players, as was Robert himself and this was also passed down and followed by his daughter Patty.

Robert and his family were prominent in the community. His military history as well as he and his sister Chella's professional success on the tennis court, was something to talk about. As we spoke for hours, it was enjoyable to hear stories of my families heritage. It was interesting to note that Mary Dowell Phillips lived with Robert and his wife for many years. Robert related stories of her days as a young child in early El Paso. He also gave me an interesting book that was written by a retired newspaper reporter in El Paso, Nancy Hamilton. The book gave an interesting history of the First Mayor of El Paso, Benjamin Shacklett Dowell. It also included a story of his life from his early days until his death in 1880.

As we spoke to Robert and his daughter, Mary Jane, as well as his daughter, Patty, over the phone, it was easy to see the love they had for each other and family. They are truly blessed and full of compassion for others. I was overjoyed with the knowledge that their inheritance from our heritage shines in their lives as it does in mine. We left them, feeling closer to an extended family and with hopes of a closer relationship. We continue our contacts with them and plan on a reunion some day, to share in the rich heritage that at one time was forsaken.

PIONEERING SPIRIT REVEALED:

As our research began to unfold, a story of a pioneering and adventurous spirit began to reveal itself. My Great Grandfather, Benjamin Shacklett Dowell was the epitome of what the Daniel Boone's and Davey Crockett's were all about. He longed for the adventure of traveling out West, from his childhood home in Kentucky.

His adventuresome spirit brought him success as well as trouble and defeat, but he never gave up. He eventually succeeded and became a legend. His many exploits were documented in many accounts of Ben Dowell's amazing life in several books.

Some of these books were: C. L. Sonnichsen's book entitled "Pass of the North" "Four Centuries on the Rio Grande", Volume l, 1968, and "Forty Years in El Paso", by W. W. Mills, 1962. Other books that were written specifically about his life, were written by Nancy Hamilton and entitled: "Ben Dowell, El Paso's First Mayor" 1976 and "Legendary Watering Holes"; "The Saloons That Made Texas Famous";

which has a chapter about Ben Dowell written by Nancy Hamilton. Louis L. Amours' "The Sackett Brand" also mentions Ben Dowell's adventurous life. He was also one of the main characters in an episode of the television show "Death Valley Days" Our research also revealed that due to Benjamin's success as the first Mayor of El Paso, and his daughter Mary being the first Anglo teacher, they were recognized by the El Paso Board of Education by naming a school after him.

The grammar school was named the Ben S Dowell School and is located at 5249 Bastille Avenue in El Paso where it stands today. Our visit to the school was one of the highlights of our trip to El Paso. We found the school in a nice, middle class section of town. The school was large with a huge sign reading "Ben S Dowell School".

The sight was heart-warming as I realized it was named after my Great Grandfather. I quickly went inside and approached the front desk in the administration building. I didn't quite know how to introduce myself and why I was there. I began to emotionally express myself as the great grandson of Benjamin Shacklett Dowell, who the school was dedicated to and named after. That was all that was needed to be said; as teachers began to appear seemingly out of nowhere. I was surrounded and surprised by interested staff, who began to discuss the fortunate chance of having a Dowell family member visit their school. I was introduced to the Superintendent of the school and welcomed with open arms, as they swarmed around me. In an embarrassing moment, I was overtaken by emotion and tears began to well up in my eyes. I expressed my surprise and lack of knowledge of such a beautiful school being dedicated to my great grandfather.

I was offered a tour by one of the teachers, and quickly ran out to the school yard where Jane was waiting for me. We were taken to several large classrooms, where computers and the latest equipment filled the room. It was exciting and astonishing to see what a beautiful school of over four hundred children, being named after my great grandfather. After an interesting and exciting tour of the school, we left with promises to return and send a finished book of our ancestry and visit to the Ben S Dowell School.

This is his story as written by me, his Great Grandson James Robert Dowell (Elijah).

 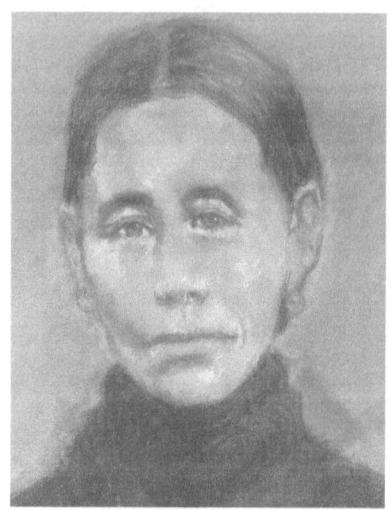

Fig. 2   Painting of Ben Dowell   Fig. 3   Painting of Juana Dowell

Fig. 4   Painting of Mary Dowell Phillips

Fig. 5   James Dowell in Front of School

Fig. 6   Side View of Ben S. Dowell School

17

CHAPTER III

THE SEARCH CONTINUES

Once Jane and I researched all the material we had from our trip to El Paso, it was plain to see that much was missing. We didn't know anything about Ben's childhood, except for the fact he was born in Meade County, Kentucky. We realized that in order to get the information we needed to complete our story on Benjamin's life, as well as other relatives living in Kentucky, we were going to have to go there! This would require a trip of several days and a rental car to get around, as well as a round trip flight. The information we had to go on was just that records indicated that Benjamin took a trip back to his childhood home in Kentucky in 1860.

During his trip he visited many family members who lived in Meade County, Kentucky near Louisville. As he visited his father, mother as well as brothers, sisters and old friends, they listened to his tales of adventure. The story that was passed down, was that he went from farm to farm accepting dinner invitations from all who wanted to see him. He placed his daughter in the saddle with him and rode his horse to all the visits. In a comment by Ben, he said that Meade County was full of Dowell's! In some contacts that we made by e-mail, a few distant relatives indicated that there were many Dowell's still living in Meade County, Kentucky.

The decision to take a trip to Kentucky was a necessary one, if we were going to find further information about Benjamin's childhood and family. The opportunity availed itself a few months later, when the school I was working for had let out for the summer. I have Jane to thank for scheduling the round trip air flight, as well as hotel, and car rental. The trip took some planning with what to take, if and when we made contact with family, we wanted to show pictures and newspaper clippings of the Dowell-Phillips family in El Paso, Texas as well as our family in California.

The date of our departure arrived with us prepared and excited about going to Kentucky. The trip would take eight hours with a layover in Houston, Texas. We anxiously boarded the plane in Ontario, California and the flight was uneventful except for a late start. This left us scrambling for our connecting flight, as we were late in arriving in Houston. It was a mad scramble, as we departed our arriving flight and walked, took the people mover, as well as escalators to our awaiting plane. The plane was a small commuter type and full of waiting passengers, who were upset over having to wait for us. The short two hour flight to Louisville, Kentucky, was crowded and unpleasant, but we arrived safely. That was the important part!

Upon arriving at the airport, it was bustling with hundreds of people seeking their flights. Once we obtained our luggage, we headed for the car rental and stood in line.

It appeared that we would be there for a while, as we became anxious to proceed with our trip. I couldn't wait to at least check a phone book to see if there were any Dowell's listed in Louisville. I asked Jane to please watch the luggage, while I looked for a phonebook. The outcome was astonishing, I saw at least twenty Dowell's listed in the

Louisville area. I returned to where Jane was, wearing a smile. I happily gave her the news and she reminded me of what had taken place in El Paso, Texas. She described how the Dowell's listed in the phone book there, either stated they weren't related, or didn't care either way. Once we left the airport, we got a glimpse of what Americana looked like in Kentucky. The few things that stood out was the size of the people, we noticed that they appeared large in stature, not necessarily fat, but large framed. There appeared to be many large families and many mixed marriages. This was noted throughout our trip, wherever we went in Louisville and around parts of Kentucky. The people were mostly friendly and helpful, as we asked for directions around town.

The other interesting thing we noticed was the muggy, humid weather we had heard about. When we arrived at our hotel, I tried to control my exuberance as I knew Jane was right about Dowell names in the phonebook, which proved itself later that night as we settled in our room. I grabbed the phone book and began making calls. I experienced the same situation we had in El Paso. The many calls I made resulted in "sorry, we aren't related" to "let me check with my grandfather, when I see him next time". Just as my wife, Jane, had said earlier, "it's not going to be that easy." After a discussion on how to find older relatives who cared to be found, we decided to go to Meade County which was a few hours away. This was where the Dowell's were described as living as far back as the late 1700's.

The following morning, we started our trip, which was a beautiful drive, through thick forests and rolling hills. The Ohio River crossed this area with long bridges over it in many places. As we proceeded through Meade County, we said a little prayer, that our trip would be successful and we would find lost heritage in the form of current Dowell families still living in this area. The drive through the forest came to a clearing where an old antique store called ABE's Cabin, referring to

Abraham Lincoln, was along the road. I had a hunch that the proprietor might know some Dowell's living in the area. Upon entering the large barn looking building made of logs, we saw an old man behind a counter. He was the man to ask about Dowell's I thought, as he looked as though he had lived here forever. He welcomed us to his store and suggested we look around and check out his many antiques. As my wife shopped, I asked the man how long he had been in the area, he replied "all my life!" Then he began a story of his father starting the store in the early 1920's and passing it on down to him.

I couldn't wait to ask him if he knew any Dowell's, so I did and he laughed and said, "they're all over the place." He then told me to proceed down the road a piece and look for a fork in the road. Then I was to turn right and within a short distance, I would find Melvin Dowell's Hardware. In a strange sort of way, he also said "you're too late to see him, he died two years ago." We left the store after a few more stories of his life in Kentucky, and then went to look for the hardware store to seek more information.

The store was easy to find as there was a large sign; "Dowell Hardware". We took pictures of the sign. To us, it was a sort of a landmark that represented the pioneering efforts of some of the Dowell's. We asked the owner, "where could we find our lost relatives?" He informed us of Melvin Dowell's death two years before and his purchase of the hardware store. He directed us to Melvin's wife, who lived a few miles away on Stith Road in Stith Valley. The journey from our home in California to Meade County, Kentucky appeared to be for naught. At first we thought we wouldn't find one blood relative at all.

We felt compelled to visit Gertrude Dowell, the widow of Melvin Dowell.

Although she was the closest thing to a relative we could find, we felt our condolences were in order. We soon found the house which was marked with a large sign "The Dowell Residence". The visit proved to be a good contact for other Dowell's living in the area. Mrs. Dowell was amiable and very helpful. She spoke of her past at times, as though her beloved husband Melvin, was still alive. She gave us an address of Richard Bernice Dowell, who was said to own property nearby that was handed down for generations. According to him, his father purchased it from James Board Dowell who was Benjamin's father. Richard B Dowell's property included an old Dowell Cemetery, where James Board Dowell and his wife Barbara Shacklett Dowell were buried. Her information came with a stern warning however, as her deceased husband and his cousin Richard never got along well. The visit with Gertrude turned into an enjoyable one, as she invited us to visit the pasture behind her house. As we approached the back gate, she yelled out a strange sound, and here came nine small Shetland ponies. They were beautiful and colorful. They all lined up against the fence, pushing each other as they sought her attention. It was interesting to see that she had a special name for each pony. The surprise didn't stop there, as we were guided to the barn where two other Shetland ponies had given birth a few weeks earlier. They were so small, yet ran around as though fully grown. They appeared to be dolls of sorts, as they were too small to imagine. It was easy to tell that she had strong feelings for her pets; although she complained of all the hard work it took to care for them. She indicted that she was going to have to sell some of them. We told her that if it were possible to stick one of the baby ponies in our suitcase, we would be happy to take one home! We left her home feeling that things were about to change for us. As we neared the area where the Dowell cemetery was suppose to be, we realized that we were lost. We stopped at a large house along the road to inquire within for directions. A young man came up to our car, as I was knocking on the door, as he had been in his back yard. As Jane yelled out to me from the car, he was already giving her directions to the cemetery in the area. I quickly told him who we were and why we were there. Although his name was Ross, not Dowell, he greeted us with a surprised look and said, "my mother was a Dowell!" Her name was Lucille Dowell. I let him know that I had a sister by the same name, who was deceased. As he proceeded to tell us of the Dowell's influence in the area, he directed us again to a close by cemetery which was possibly a Dowell burial ground.

The cemetery was near a house, with a chain link fence surrounding it. The burial plots appeared to be well taken care of and the headstones appeared to be over a hundred years old We found headstones with names of related families, but no Dowell's.

We found out later, that the actual Dowell cemetery had not received the same care. The next search was for Richard Bernice Dowell, who was said to be a close relative. His farm was somewhat historical as it contained a small Dowell Cemetery dating back to the early 1800's. This was the resting place for James Board Dowell and Barbara Shacklett Dowell and we were later told this land had originally been owned by James Board Dowell and sold to Richard Bernice Dowell's father prior to James's death.

As we roamed the countryside for Richard Bernice Dowell's farm, a passing car slowed down, as the driver could tell we were strangers and looking lost. He directed us to the Dowell farm, which also had a large sign with "R. B. Dowell" written on it.

It was plain to see that the Dowell's were not trying to hide! We drove into the driveway and as I got out of the car, I could see Jane was reluctant to join me, after thinking about what was said by Mrs. Gertrude Dowell. I found R. B. Dowell working on a tractor. He was a small, friendly man with a big smile and strong characteristic qualities about him. He had a proud look and gladly introduced himself. As he spoke of his knowledge of Dowell history, he reminded me of my father who was also small in stature, but very strong for his size. Although he had a guarded demeanor, he invited us into his home to meet his wife. As Jane was still in the car, I waved to her that all was O. K. and Richard continued "us Dowell's are jack of all trades! See these two houses, one I live in and one I rent" I noticed that they were large, well built homes that looked in good shape. "I built these houses!" He went on to say that he repaired his own tractors and farm equipment. He was also a farmer raising corn and alfalfa, as well as a cattle rancher with 200 head of cattle. Then as he caught his breath he said, "I also play violin at a senior community center every Friday night and I've never missed a night for thirty years." I thought to myself, after he told me he was seventy seven years old and in good health, that he was indeed an amazing person.

Once I introduced my skeptical wife to Richard, he told us to call him R. B. Then we went to the house to meet his wife. The chance meeting of such a nice couple was truly a blessing. They welcomed us with open arms. Once we were introduced to his wife, Anna Francis, it was like we were back home just visiting relatives we hadn't seen for a long time. We were truly in the right place, as our conversation took us all the way back to the early pioneering days of the 1800's. It was learned that R. B., better known as Junior, as his father was also named Richard Bernice Dowell, was a first cousin of sorts. The visit was interesting to say the least, as stories of a pioneering family known as the Dowell's settled in this area of Meade County, Kentucky two centuries before.

Before we left, we were taken through the house and shown Anna Francis's collections of animals and her antique doll and Junior's toy John Deere collection, which they were very proud of. We found it very interesting as my wife, Jane, likes to collect glass eggs and collectable plates and could relate to the enthusiasm of any type of collection. We were invited to return to a good old fashioned hoe-down, at the local Senior Citizen Community Center. This would be our chance to hear Junior play the violin and enjoy a barn dance festival, much like the one's Benjamin Dowell, my great grandfather attended. We promised to return that Friday night, and left with a satisfied feeling of having met my connection to the past.

In a light hearted conversation with Jane on our way back to Louisville, I commented on how Junior Dowell's fiddle playing encouraged me to write a book on my heritage reaching back beyond America to England, where it all began. In a bit of excitement I said "just think honey, we could have our own 'roots story', since we have our own 'fiddla.'" The suggestion brought laughter to our discussion, which was later to be closer to the truth then we realized.

As the end of our visit approached, we felt good about the contacts we made, however there was much left unanswered. I was able to see and feel what it must have been like, for my great grandfather Benjamin's childhood. He was brought up in a beautiful environment of rolling hills, thick with forests and wild game. To see many old log cabins still standing, dating back to his time, was truly awesome. It left me with a respect for what they must have gone through, as early pioneers of this magnificent country of ours. We visited some of the large caves which had a story unto themselves. One particular cave in Meade County was discovered by Daniel Boone and his brother, Squire Boone, in the 1700's. Daniel and Squire Boone lived in this cave for some time, and hid from pursuing Indians who were out to do them in. The cave was also used by Rebel soldiers hiding out from Union forces during the Civil War.

We anxiously looked forward to our invitation to the Friday night hoe-down. As we waited, we took in many tourist attractions, such as the Churchill Down's Race Track, the Louisville Slugger factory, and a ride on the steamship "Belle of Louisville". During our stay, we also took in the heritage House of local history, and the City Library, where we gathered much information concerning the Dowell and other pioneering families.

Once Friday arrived, we took the trip back to Meade County which found us lost and frantic to find the Senior Community Center where our newly found family was waiting.

We reached the large entertainment center a little late, but welcomed never the less. To see Junior Dowell and his wife Anna Francis all dressed up and enjoying a festive occasion they have enjoyed for thirty five years, was memorable. We danced to the fiddle playing of Junior and watched the old fashioned square dancing that was reminiscent of the early pioneer days. As the dance "caller" yelled out the steps to the dancers who joined hands, it brought back highlights of what it must have been like in the early years in Kentucky. We took many pictures and met many friends of the Dowell's. It was a night we will remember, as happy dancers re-connected with their past ancestors by re-living the dances and festive gatherings of their Kentucky past. As we bid farewell to our Kentucky family, we promised to return some day and continue our friendship. We also exchanged phone numbers and addresses and agreed to keep in touch.

The last few days of our unforgettable trip, still left us yearning to learn more of the Dowell history. We made an effort to reach our cousin, William (Bill) Dowell of Virginia by e-mail from the hotel and let him know our dilemma. It was the next to the last day of our departure home, when we received the news from Bill. He was surprised to hear we were in Kentucky and asked us if we were able to find Mark Dowell, a relative of ours. He lived in Louisville and exchanged family tree information with Bill for many years. He was said to be very interested in the Dowell history in America as well as in

England, the country of our origin. The chance of meeting a relative who had taken such an active part in researching and compiling Dowell history was indeed something to be excited about.

Our contact with Mark was pleasant and helpful, as he invited us to his home and later led us to his computer. It was plain to see that he spent much time seeking records and information on the Dowell history. The visit with him and his two boys was short, but interesting and enjoyable. Unfortunately, we didn't get a chance to meet his wife as she was working. The real shock of the visit, was when Mark gave us reams and reams of Dowell history and the family tree. It was astonishing to say the least. The information Mark and Bill had gathered over the years was truly a work of art. It gave stories and concise records of a family tree that went all the way back to England. One story which was documented and based on fact was that my GGGGGG Grandfather William Dowell came to America from England as an indentured servant to John Hancock, when he was twelve.

The acceptance by such nice people, who invited us into their homes, was very satisfying. The information we received from Mark, left me with a desire to write about our families heritage all the way back to England. The common thread that seemed to run through my families history, was a strong faith in and love of God and Country. They brought the Lord with them in their heart, mind and soul as well as their bible. This was observed in the current families in Kentucky and El Paso, Texas, as well as in documented stories of the early pioneers.

As we left Kentucky, with our treasure of information, it was satisfying to have enjoyed a great vacation, and at the same time visit with previously unknown family.

I couldn't wait to start my book on my heritage, because now I was planning on writing a story going all the way back to jolly old England. This would be quite an undertaking,but well worth it. To go from an unknown ancestry to a heritage from across the sea, would be a dream come true. My search and hunger for heritage has finally been met thanks to "family" in Texas and Kentucky. My trips were well worth the time and energy. It is my desire that others in this large family of mine will find enjoyment in my book and have a little more knowledge about the "Dowell's of Kentucky" and "Dowell's of Texas", and "Dowell's of California".

Fig. 7 Abe's Country Store

Fig. 8   James and Jane Dowell and Richard Bernice Dowell
and wife Anna Francis

Fig. 9   Richard Bernice Dowell (Junior)

Fig. 10   Hardware Store Originally Owned by
Melvin H. Dowell visited by James R. Dowell

Fig. 11   Melvin H. Dowell B-Feb. 20, 1936 D-July 9, 2003
Spouse, Geraldine, Still Living in Family Home

CHAPTER IV

A FATHERLESS CHILDHOOD CREATES AN ANGRY CHILD

The many years of a lifetime of no knowledge of my father's past ancestry, left me anxious to discover the truth. Thanks to my tenacious and determined wife Jane, a breakthrough came through several weeks after the search began. As the pieces began to fit, it left us with hope that eventually we would discover my father's past.

The history of my father's past revealed that he was fatherless for most of his childhood. His father, Elijah Dowell was incarcerated in a prison in Huntsville, Texas for stealing a horse. The record showed he had fought the allegations and testified "not guilty". He was found guilty by a court of law and sentenced to five years in prison. Elijah began his sentence ten days before his son, my father, Edward Dowell was born. The prison records indicated that Elijah was married with no children. This was due to the fact that his son Edward had not been born as yet. The search for his mother began, as nothing we could find would give us any clues. What we did discover at the time, was that my father was born in Ft. Davis, Texas, on July 7, 1895. This was a surprise to us, as we thought he was born near El Paso, as this was where Elijah was raised and thought to have lived most of his younger life.

The search for my father's mother became a laughable situation, as my wife Jane would discover a new possibility every now and then. I would hear a loud yell from her as she searched our ancestry "your Grandmother was so and so" and then a pause as she pounded her computer keyboard and retracted her statement! As she progressed through the many possibilities, it left my father with several mothers. In our minds, it was like we felt "would the real mother please stand up!" The frustration began to grip us as we continued to draw a losing hand. I strained my brain trying to come up with any relatives who were still alive that may know something. I called my ninety five year old Aunt who was married to my deceased Uncle. She couldn't remember what she did yesterday, let alone who was who years and years earlier. As I questioned all my sisters and brothers again, for the tenth time looking for clues, it became apparent that we weren't going to get anywhere with what little information they had.

We were facing a blank past as we looked for Mrs. Elijah Dowell. Then a continued search began to isolate two potential names, a Fannie and a Violet. It had been discovered by this time, that Elijah had been married twice. Could it be that both women were wives of Elijah at one time or another? I began to miss the excited yells coming from Jane's computer room, as she continued to look for my grandmother.

No response from her simply meant she found nothing more. Then as quietly as it began, I looked up from the dinner table and stared at Jane, who was holding a freshly printed copy from her computer in her hand. She was quietly standing over me, with a sheepish grin on her face. I took the copy from her outstretched hand and began to read. The following story began to come together as tears filled my eyes. My father suffered through a fatherless and sometimes motherless childhood.

The marriage between Elijah and Fannie Dowell took place on or around 1895, the same year he was placed in a Texas prison. My father was fatherless for most of his childhood. His mother Fannie, did the best she could for a young girl of twenty two. The stories we had heard of my dad being brought up by neighbors must have been true! The neighbors of that day would help each other when needed. Obviously, Fannie was in need. She had to work to provide for her son and herself. It was apparent that my father had many mothers of sorts, as neighbors would pitch in to help Fannie, while she worked.

The release of Elijah from prison in 1900 made no difference in my dad's life as he never returned to him at the time. It is not known whether he couldn't find him or just chose to forget him. In 1903 my dad's future stepfather returned from the Philippines and several years in the Military. Milton Tinney then met Fannie and her son, Edward, and they married sometime in the early 1900's. They lived for many years in Corpus Christi as revealed by a 1910 census showing Milton Tinney as head of household, Fannie as his wife and Edward Dowell as his stepson. The strain of a step father who apparently put up with him to remain married to Fannie was more than my dad could stand. This relationship explained the stories we had heard that my dad was adopted. His given name was not changed however and he remained a Dowell. A few years after Elijah's release from the Huntsville Prison he married Violet, who had a son named Ed L. L. Perry from a previous marriage.

This made sense to us, as there was a story that Elijah had a stepson. His stepson was through his second marriage and had nothing to do with my father being adopted.

There was no record of whatever happened to Violet and her son, but sometime later Elijah was alone again and possibly ill. There were stories that his wife Violet died at an early age. The story didn't end there however. Elijah eventually returned to his son Edward and renewed their relationship. The records show that my dad and his father reunited sometime between 1910 and 1917. This could have occurred due to Elijah's illness as the records indicate in a Military Draft registration notice filed by my dad, stating he was taking care of his father at that time. A census report taken in 1920 revealed that Edward Dowell and his wife Estella Dominguez Dowell, along with his father Elijah Dowell were living together in Lakewood, New Mexico.

According to my older brothers and sisters, they recall our grandpa living near them in Lakewood, New Mexico, in the early 1930's. He would bring them sacks of fruit and vegetables from the local fields and throw aways behind local grocery stores. He could be seen carrying a large burlap sack over his shoulder full of fruit and goodies for them, down the road as he approached the house. This was how they remember their Grandpa Elijah.

Elijah passed away on December 15, 1937 after a long stay in a hospital in Carlsbad, New Mexico. All the family attended the funeral of their beloved Grandpa Elijah, the only one that dad spoke of when he talked of his past. So ends the story of Elijah Dowell, my grandpa. He lived a quiet, simple life leaving little to speak of, but never forgetting his rightful son. Once I was able to know and understand my father's past, it was easier to understand why he was the way he was.

The critical years of a child's life when a mother and father are so important, was lacking in my father's childhood. He was tossed around from neighbor to neighbor. With a father in prison and a desperate young mother, the years were hard as she struggled to survive and care for her child. The lack of proper parental care and feeling lost and unloved, took its toll on my father's feelings about life. He grew up without the ability to show compassion and love for others, as he struggled to make sense of it all. His childhood and young life left him drained emotionally, and without any feelings for his mother. The final blow came when his mother married a man my father never cared for. The little attention he was accustomed to totally ended as she gave all her time to her husband. My father left home as soon as he was able and started his own life.

I have long since forgiven my father for his lack of fatherly love and concern. He just didn't know how to hug a child and say "I love you". He lived what he was taught.

CHAPTER V

THE FIRST SETTLERS OF MEADE COUNTY, KENTUCKY

Although Benjamin's story was amazing in itself, it is noted that his ancestors were just as amazing. Their stories of heroism and pioneering feats were examples that Benjamin embraced in his quest for his own glory, as they followed the like of Daniel and his brother, Squire Boone, into the wilderness.

In the mid 1700's, Daniel Boone was exploring the Northern part of Kentucky. His younger brother, Squire Boone, followed his footsteps into the wild Mid-West. One of the journeys Squire took was to Northern Kentucky, where Meade County is today. His discovery of a spring and some large caves in this area are now tourist attractions. Prior to specific names given to this region, descriptions were; "a high ridge at a pond" and "sugar tree". Other descriptions were; " at the mouth of Wolf Creek" or "Boone Spring near Big Spring".

In 1780, Daniel Boone built a hunting camp and planted a patch of ground at Boone Spring, named after himself of course. Land was purchased using Boone's Spring as a landmark in 1793. Tracts named "Bulger Grove", "Tomahawk Mark", and "Blue Ball" began to emerge.

Later, the names of Doe Run, Sulpher Grove, Deer Lick, Four Springs, and Oak Grove began to appear. These names still exist today. The evidence of the oldest settlement made by white men in Meade County was at the mouth of Wolf Creek. The first permanent settlements in Meade County, Kentucky were made in Hill Grove, Stith Valley, Doe Run, and Otter Creek.

In 1784, Richard Stith, born 1727 and Lucy Hall Stith born 1736 settled in Stith Valley. They were married in Virginia, December 28, 1756 and were the parents of twelve children. Their son, Joseph Stith born September 6, 1759, was a soldier in the Revolutionary War. Many of the Stith's children later married into the Dowell family.

As the patents were granted , tracts of land attracted immigrants from many areas who began to move in, especially from Virginia. Other descendants who moved to Stith Valley were the Shacklett family. They were of French origin and according to entries recorded in a Bible owned by Benjamin Woodbridge Shacklett, the following took place; the migration to America occurred sometime around the 1700's. Benjamin (Wooley) Shacklett's father, John Shacklett, was born in Virginia in 1747. Benjamin was born in Pennsylvania in 1774. After the death of Benjamin's father, John Shacklett, his will was probated in Fayette County, Pennsylvania. The will provided for the widow and the children. Benjamin (Wooley) Shacklett was appointed one of the executors and was sworn in on March 1, 1810. After the estate was settled, their children moved to Meade County, Kentucky. They landed at Soloman Brandenburg's Ferry in Meade County. The name at the time was "Buzzard Roost". They brought all their household goods as well as stock and supplies with them. This included castings, bar irons, axes, hoes, reaping hooks and some square box stoves, the first ever introduced to the county. They paid for their land with bar iron castings and mill stones, they quarried themselves from their father's quarry in Pennsylvania.

In records written around 1800, Benjamin Woodbridge (Wooley) Shacklett tells the following story. "After the death of my grandfather, my grandmother rode on horseback from near Beastontown, Pennsylvania, to Meade County, Kentucky where we lived. She brought her youngest son with her, which was a trip upward of 500 miles. Her age was 64 at the time. She was 97 years of age when she died. She was buried on the high ground of Hill Grove."

Another family who migrated to Meade County was John and Roxina Kirkpatrick Wimp. They followed the Shacklett's on their journey to Kentucky. The Wimp family parents were from Ireland where they were married. He served as a Sergeant in Captain James Floyd's Company of Cumberland County, Pennsylvania in April 23, 1779, in the Revolutionary War. One of their children, Polly Wimp, was later to marry George Dowell. John Wimp was well educated. He joined the Masonic Order in Europe. He frequently spoke of having met George Washington in the Masonic Lodge at Fairfax, Pennsylvania. He had a Masonic medal which he greatly prized, having brought it from the old country. He tied it around his neck and was buried with it, as requested, at Hill Grove, Kentucky. He died at the age of ninety eight.

The Dowell family, Elijah Dowell and his wife Jemima Board Dowell as well as their children left Bedford County, Virginia and moved to Meade County around 1810. Their son, James Board Dowell was born on May 15, 1791, in Bedford County, Virginia. He was married by Simon Buchanan on February 8, 1813, to Barbara Shacklett who was born April 26, 1794, in Fayette County, Pennsylvania. They were married in Ekron/Garnetsville, Meade County, Kentucky. Barbara Shacklett was the daughter of Benjamin Woodbridge (Wooley)

Shacklett, and Elizabeth Ashcraft. James Board Dowell was a Veteran of the War of 1812 and served in the Hopkins Campaign.

He was the first Captain of Patrollers for Meade County, Kentucky. The Patrollers included Benjamin Shaver, Daniel Fulton, Lewis Walker and Daniel Shacklett (1824).

James Board Dowell lived in Jackey's Grove along with Jacob Hayden in 1824. James occupation was a farmer. In religion he was a free thinker and anticlerical.

Barbara Shacklett was a self-taught doctor and a founding member of the Hill Grove Baptist Church. They had twelve children. Both are buried on their old farm which is now owned by Richard Bernice Dowell (Junior), in Stith Valley, near Guston, Meade County, Kentucky.

The settling of Kentucky came at a high price. Between 1783 to 1790, 1500 people fell victim to savage Indian attacks, according to historical records. Another well known explorer was Richard Ashcraft, from Pennsylvania. The Ashcraft's had built a fort in Pennsylvania prior to moving to Meade County, Kentucky. Absalom and Abisha Ashcraft were also part of the family who led the way for settlers in Kentucky. The area known as Meade County, was named after Captain James Meade, who was killed in the battle of River Raisen, during the Revolutionary War. Life was much more simple in those days, than it is now. The pioneers needs were few. A small patch of land was all an average family needed, usually around three acres to grow crops and raise stock. A list of property to be presented for taxing was written in 1826-1827 by James Mc Ououn. The property listed were: 318 acres of land $318.00, two blacks Total $400.00, one horse beast $50.00 for a grand total of $768.00. Also included were one kettle, three pots, teapot, coffeepot, 2 dozen plates, a basin, two axes, an iron, sixteen hogs, two cows, eight sheep, twelve poultry, large fireplace. This was considered to be a well to do farmer, during this era. As settlers tilled the soil and planted crops, as well as raise their stock, the farms grew in size and stature. It was stated that General Benjamin Shacklett, one of the first settlers in Hill Grove in an account in the Hayden's Family book, had several hundred deer skins to tan and sell that he had trapped and killed. In one story of the Shacklett Family, Bancet Shacklett was known as a great bear hunter, he had shot a bear that continued to run and hide in a cave. It had gotten dark so he persuaded his wife to follow him into the cave, holding a torch. Since she had such faith in his hunting skills, she held the torch while he found the bear and killed it. The fondness for a small bear pet, almost cost them their daughter, Sophia's life. The bear grew and eventually broke the chain restraining it. The bear mauled their daughter and came close to killing her.

In written memoirs of William G. Bell, another Meade County settler, he stated, "Benjamin Shacklett stayed at my house one night and told me of many of his adventures.' Ben said, "the woods were full of wild game where I hunted in 1832 throughout the Meade County area." In other stories he related how marauding Indians would scalp any settlers they could find. In one situation where the Indians killed a family, they found two children hidden under a cabin floor. The Indians kept the two children for over two years until they were sold back to a Colonel John Hardin. There were many Indian fights between 1791 and 1794. In one of the last skirmishes, an Indian had stopped to get water near Jordon Springs. He was seen by some white hunters who shot and killed him.

The collective efforts of many families built churches and schools which later became the first sign of a town. In that day, no teacher ever thought of conducting a school without the rod as one of the pieces of furniture of the school room. The switch was made of a nice slim limb of beech, three to five feet long. It was roasted or warmed in the stove, so it would not easily break. When properly prepared, it would lap over the shoulder and down the back, all around the victim, without breaking. Its use was common and over half the male students felt its sting almost daily.

The social interaction among the early families of Meade County was exemplified by their unique gatherings, where self-taught banjo and fiddle players as well as harmonica sounds were heard, not to mention spoon rattling, tin kettles and poker tongs.

The small makeshift musical groups would entertain the local citizenry, as they danced to square dancing reels, jigs, and heel tapping. The children of that day found and created their own games like hide and seek, jump rope, hopscotch, marbles and ring around the roses. These games continue to amuse children of today. The simple but alluring past time also included crawdad, bullfrog and fish, fishing. These playtime and social gatherings gave the early pioneers a means of relaxing and enjoying each others company. There were many a night when neighborhood families gathered around a large bonfire to tell stories of heroic deeds and wild adventures of their predecessors. In stories handed down, it was not uncommon to hear of great Indian fighters like Daniel Boone and his brother, Squire, as well as others. The attacks by savages and wild beasts that ravaged the trail blazers and their kin, brought tears to the listening crowds.

The pioneering families of Kentucky had some very tough and determined ancestors who were brave, hard working, common people who gave totally of themselves to bring peace, tranquility and the love of God and Country to this wild, untamed land. They paid the price for what later was to become the most beautiful and bountiful country in the world. Since the early pioneers were usually living miles apart, just seeing another human being was a pleasure for them. It provided a break from the loneliness of backwoods life. They always kept their doors open to anyone who needed a place to stay. Pioneers always had food on hand to offer unexpected guests.

Sometimes, guest were allowed to stay over night. Their world of fun was founded on human relationships. Friendship was one of their highest values in life. Once there was friendship, their imagination provided the pleasures and pastimes. Out of caring, sharing and cooperation, came a wonderful world of pleasure that no gadget today could possibly replace.

Some simple pleasures pioneers found in their lives were the smell of homemade bread, the sight of the first bloom in spring, and the sound of a babbling brook. If trees could talk, they would probably tell stories of children skipping rope, of women quilting in the shade, and of young men arm wrestling for the title of village champion.

The children used to claim that their grandmothers jam was the sweetest, their grandfathers fruit the most juicy, and their mothers garden filled with the most colorful flowers imaginable. The beauty of unspoiled nature was a daily pleasure to their senses. The home was the center of early pioneer life. These families spent their happiest times under their own roof talking to people and laughing around the fireplace.

The pioneers would gather around their kitchen fireplace after dinner each night and share the days experiences or listen to grandpa talk about the days when he was a young boy. Even after they had candles, they sat in one room reading, sewing, or playing.

The families were very close in those days and parents spent every evening with their children. One of the biggest joys of life was being with people you love.

The barnyard animals were also a bit of joy, once the work was done. These animals provided work, milk, food and even companionship. The whole pioneer household would await anxiously for a new calf or foal to be born. Baby pigs and goats were always fun to be around. Witnessing the miracle of new life was a regular happening in their household. They were grateful for their success in the new world.

They offered prayers of thanks for each day of happiness. They asked for God's help to stay healthy and strong. Sunday was a special day. It was a day of rest and prayer for adults and children alike. Sunday was reserved for reading the Bible. Bible stories gave the pioneers advice in times of trouble and examples of courage and resourcefulness.

The childhood history and pioneers way of life, describes the way Benjamin Shacklett Dowell was raised as a child and young man in his growing years in Meade County, Kentucky. This resulted in a strong character of love and compassion for his fellowman. His love of family, God, and Country were established at a young age. He lived this philosophy throughout his adventurous life.

Fig. 12   Family Reunion Every Year at Daniel Boone's Doe Run Inn

Fig. 13   Creek Behind Doe Run Inn

Fig. 14   Boone's Mill Preserved as it is Today

Fig. 15   Daniel Boone's Mill Today (Built in 1809) Backside

Fig. 16   Squire Boone Cave Today

Chapter VI

Their Coming to America

The end of the Revolutionary War brought freedom and liberty to all. The tyranny of the King of England and the persecution by the church was no longer an issue in America. The heroic battle brought a renewed faith in God and a promise of a better place to live. The passion to be free from taxation without representation. . . .free to speak one's mind and live one's dreams was the cry from all who lived in this country of freedom. "America" was now the ultimate hope of making a new country, unlike any the world had ever known. The limits of what we could do and be were set by our own willingness to bring all of our ability to create the life we chose. The escape from tyranny and persecution was so great, so wonderful, that very few who came here ever chose to return to their land of origin.

"America" drew immigrants by the thousands from all over the world, as early as the 1700's. the lure of a better life with riches beyond anyone could imagine, began to fire up the spirit of adventure in many hearts across Europe. Only the strong and spiritually driven were fit to take the journey across the shores to America. They were motivated by the chance to make a new life for themselves, free of harassment by the church. The fear of never seeing their loved one's again, and separation from their place of birth was overcome by their desire for a new life, a promise of freedom and free will to be able to raise their families without fear of government intrusion.

This was the setting that brought the Dowell's and thousands of other families to the new world of "America", from England.

Their journey to America took on many different ways to seek passage to the new world. One documented journey on record from Surry County, Virginia, revealed that my G G G G G G Grandfather, William Dowell was born in Painswick, England in the year 1683.

According to records from Surry County, Virginia Colonist, he came to the Colony on the ship Hampshire as an indentured servant to John Hancock in 1695 at the age of twelve.

Other records indicate he was on the south side of Nattowat in 1714. William was located in records of Dettingen Parish, Prince William County, Virginia in December of 1756, where he had awarded his son, Thomas, 267 pounds of tobacco in return for caring for him in his old age. It is believed that William died in Prince William County, Virginia not long after this award to Thomas. It is not known at this time who William's bride was or the number of children they may have had.

The passage for a trip from England to America was very expensive. This generally required the need for all of the family's property to be sold, as well as the use of any savings they may have had. Although none of our ancestors were lost at sea as they came across the Atlantic according to records, the trip was dangerous and at times treacherous. Once immigrants of the early era arrived in the Virginia Colonies, they were subject to unscrupulous manipulation and fraudulent businessmen who misguided them for their own gain. The result was loss of any funds or property they brought with them, until they became familiar with the appropriate channels of seeking temporary lodging and passage out of Virginia to the outlying areas. Once they began to settle in Kentucky and other states, they had Indians and other problems to deal with. They overcame their difficulties, and small towns and farms began to turn into communities of safe haven and prosperous endeavors.

The early pioneers who came to the Midwest during this period of migration,were a tough lot. They were willing to fight the remaining Indians for their place in the new world. The hazards of living in a new territory, with storms and floods they were unfamiliar with, created the challenge of their lives. Their strength and direction was ingrained in a deep belief of the saving grace of God. They brought Him with them in their hearts, their books and their minds. This strong spiritual connection, and the deep well of faith in the Lord that all would be right and safe on their difficult journey and settlement in the new land, gave them the will to succeed.

The churches of their chosen faith, Baptist, Methodist and Catholic as well as other denominations, began to spring up all around the country. In many cases, the local church's became the town-hall meeting place where many of the town folk, as well as the farmers, would get together to discuss mutual problems. This abiding faith gave them the compassion to help one another, as troubles and hazards befell them. They grouped together to overcome the obstacles and suffered and laughed together as things began to improve. Out of their pain and suffering, as well as success, came the mighty and strong country of "America". As the call went out across this beautiful land of ours; "God bless America, long may she live!"

The Kentucky frontier was an oasis for the early settlers and explorers. The land was a veritable hunters paradise. The buffalo, antelope, deer and bears were plentiful.

These beautiful beasts knew no fear of man's encroachment, as they roamed the stretches of forest throughout Kentucky. The early explorers like Daniel Boone and his brother Squire, found the awesome Kentucky river, fed by its many branches of streams and rainfall. They marveled at the endless prairie and hundreds of wild turkeys, thousands of pigeons, woodchucks and squirrels in every tree. The forests were full of berries, blue grass, clover, fruits and nuts, it was like a dream. The rivers, creeks and waterways were filled with an abundance of fish. This abundance of game and wildlife was what greeted the early settlers of Kentucky and surrounding states.

The Indians' Iroquois and Shawnee as well as other tribes, were not as much a threat when settlers began to appear, as they were in Daniel Boone and his brother Squire's day. As settlers arrived, the Indians fled to places further west and deeper into the forest. The Kentucky landscape became a peaceful area and the Meade County valleys were a welcoming place for the Dowell's and many other families drawn to this area.

Chapter VII

Young Ben

The date was the 1800's and all was at peace in the world. The place was Meade County, Kentucky, near the Ohio river. These were the growing years for the young State of Kentucky. The plantations and farms were large and crops were plentiful as well as barns full of animals. The best being Kentucky bred racing horses, who roamed the blue grass pastures of the state. The families who moved into Meade County, Kentucky were friendly and large. Many came from the nearby states of Virginia, North and South Carolina as well as Tennessee. As for the Dowell and Shacklett families, they were from Virginia and could be traced all the way back to Yorkshire, England in the 1700's. These large, close knit families that lived in the green hills and valleys near the Ohio River, were the Hayden's, the Wimp's, the Shacklett's, the Taylor's and the Stith's from Stith Valley.

The close ties among the families brought the beautiful Barbara Shacklett and the handsome James Board Dowell to union in early 1812. Their wedding was the talk of the town as they grew up near each other in the town called Louisville. Their marriage was blessed with twelve children, one of which was my Great Grandfather, Benjamin Shacklett Dowell their fifth child born November 30, 1818.

Ben as he was called, lived a Tom Sawyer type of childhood as he loved the outdoors and the beauty of the country side that made up the Midwest. He would ride his horse for miles, as a young boy along the Ohio River. The flat boats carrying supplies down river from Louisville to Paducah, Kentucky and on down to the Mississippi River and all the way to Nachez, Louisiana were exciting to watch. The boats men would stop their large barges along the river and camp out for the night. Ben would come along by the river bank and listen to their stories of adventure, as they spoke of magnificent mountains and flat green plains as far as the eye could see! The amazing sights Ben would hear about, left him filled with the spirit of adventure. As a young teenage boy, he would dream of a day when he would be able to join a wagon train headed for the West.

Although Ben enjoyed his family life, with many brothers and sisters, he longed for more than the Kentucky countryside had to offer. His younger years were filled with camping and hunting trips he would take with his father and brothers. He learned to fire a rifle at a young age and had a horse as soon as he was able to be placed in a saddle. The wild game of deer, buffalo, wild turkeys as well as rabbits, quail and fish made it a paradise for hunting and fishing. This life suited Ben as he grew up living a pioneers dream of exploration and love for the great outdoors.

Just like many young boys his age, there were many chores to do around the farm. He helped feed the livestock, work the crops and repair broken fences. As soon as there was free time, he was outdoors chasing wild game on his horse. This was where he felt he belonged. The years were kind to Ben on his father's farm, as it grew and prospered. They raised cattle and horses, as well as many crops like corn, alfalfa and wheat as well as tobacco. The early pioneers of this area would all get together on occasion and have a good old fashion hoe-down. The barn dance was also a place to get together to discuss their farms, and for the young boys, a chance to meet some pretty girls.

As Ben grew older, he was well trained in all aspects of farming, hunting and exploring the wooded forests. He was a good looking, hard working type of guy, who was considered a good candidate for any young girl looking for a man who would care for her and give her a home to be proud of. The courtship of Ben and the beautiful Melvina Stith from Stith Valley was no surprise to many of the local families. The few large families of the Meade County area, intermarried as convenience, closeness and similar life styles gave way to romantic attraction.

Since the area began to flourish with large farms and social culture, it brought prominence, wealth and stature to the many families living in the area. There were the Stith family from Stith Valley who raised several beautiful daughters, that caught the eye of Benjamin Dowell and his two younger brothers, John and James who married Stith girls as they reached their twenties. Benjamin Dowell was married to Melvina Stith just twenty days past his twentieth birthday on December 20th 1838. The marriage was destined for failure as Benjamin Dowell was an adventurous soul,where his wife Melvina was a more settled person.

Ben's love of horses and where they could take him, began to give him itchy feet to travel and see the world. His parents were a prominent, well to do family and this gave Benjamin the opportunity to grow up at an early age and experience life as he traveled about the country side. He watched his father run a large farm with many horses and other animals. He customarily wore the cowboy wear of the time; jeans, vests and boots, but was required to dress up and present a young gentleman who reflected the prominence of the Dowell family at social functions. This was encouraged by his gentleman farmer father and social elite mother who displayed their proud heritage and place in the community.

Is it any wonder that Benjamin was drawn to the beautiful Melvina Stith who came from a wealthy landowner in Stith Valley.

The marriage was a culmination of close prominent families that socialized much together and brought their children up with dignity, character and the desire for the good things in life. Although Ben enjoyed the social life that wealth had to offer, with family gatherings, picnics and festive affairs, his real longing was for the adventure of traveling to the West and seeing the other side of the mountains. His family, friends and wife, Melvina, tried their best to tame his wild side and desire he had to travel. His father James, attempted to show him what would be his some day if he remained in Kentucky with his family. But try as they may, Benjamin had a wondering soul and looked for suitable ways to seek adventure.

The opportunity came when President Polk told Congress that Mexico had invaded the United States and American blood had been shed on American soil. The Mexican American War began on May 13, 1846 when Congress declared war and Major General Zachary Taylor started his drive into Mexico.

By June 9, 1846 Benjamin was in Louisville signing up with the Kentuckians in the Volunteers. He was assigned as a Private to Captain Aaron Pennington's Company G in Colonel Humphrey Marshall's first regiment, Kentucky Calvary. His last visit to his family before he left was to say goodbye, as he left his wife, family and friends behind. His parents were proud of him, however, and admired the way he looked in uniform sitting erect, tall and slim on his horse as came naturally for a Kentuckian. They would miss his gentle smile, and his clear blue eyes that could twinkle with good humor or turn steely in quiet opposition. They would wonder often about Benjamin in the years to come, as he spent months in a Mexican prison.

Benjamin was among 200,000 men who answered the call to arms within a few days of the declaration of war. He took with him a $50 horse and $20 worth of equipment. The volunteers were sent to the Rio Grande to join General Taylor, whose goal was Monterey, the opening to the heart of Mexico, a move which began in early August 1846. Of General Taylor's 6,600 men, about half were volunteers. The First Kentucky Regiment and the First Ohio formed the First Brigade, which was commanded by General William Hamer.

On September 18, 1846 as the advance began on Monterey, the First Kentucky was used to support the Mortar and howitzer battery as other units dispersed to points in town. They remained there several weeks after their victory, until General Taylor began moving again on November 13, 1846, this time toward Saltillo. By January 1st they could claim three more victories over Mexican forces.

Benjamin Dowell was riding in a patrol of Kentuckians about fifty miles south of Saltillo on January 21, 1847 when a downpour drove the men to seek cover at the hacienda called "La Encarnacion". A similar patrol of Arkansas men also waited out the storm there. Being volunteers, they neglected the military custom of sending out scouts to patrol the surrounding area. At dawn, Benjamin and the other soldiers were awakened to the sound of a loud bugle and the shouts of "charge", yelled out in Spanish by General Vincente Minon's troops, it was too late to do anything except surrender.

The Kentucky troops could see they were completely surrounded by hundreds of Santa Ana's soldiers. They all knew that the attempt to fight would be suicide, as they would be cut down by the soldiers that out numbered them ten to one. Their Commanding General, William Hamer, yelled out to them "lay down your arms!" The indignation of giving up without a fight could be seen on everyone's face, as they dropped their rifles and silently stood by, as Mexican troops poured into the hacienda. The Mexican soldiers were yelling out obscenities and hitting some of Ben's comrades with the butt of their rifles. There was no reason for this action, as all of them complied with the order to surrender. It was simply to show them who was the boss! Once Ben was lined up in the hacienda yard along with all the American troops, they were stripped of anything that could be used as a weapon and forced to remain standing in the hot sun all day. They were forced to lie on the cold ground that night, uncovered as Mexican soldiers insured that their blankets were free from any contraband. After a miserably cold night on the ground, they were awaken at daybreak and forced to begin their long march to Mexico City.

As Ben began to hear the soldiers talk about heading for Mexico City, it became clear to him that he may never see his loved one's again. He was one of a few men who could understand Spanish at the time, having learned it from neighbor kids, when he lived in Kentucky. The sad news was not something he wanted to tell his friends and fellow soldiers, as they were under enough strain as it was and this bad news would only depress them more. Although Ben could hear their captors talk about their fate, some saying most of the prisoners would not make it to Mexico City alive! It was what Ben saw that surprised him more, the Mexican soldiers were as poorly fed as they were. There were many who were sick and dying from dysentery, typhus and lack of proper medicine. The sick Mexican soldiers who were bordering on death were left behind to care for themselves. It appeared that more of them would die as they journeyed to Mexico City.

Although Benjamin had nothing good to relate to his fellow soldiers, he knew that he had to try and make them feel that rescue was on the way. It was important to keep their spirits up, or they could succumb to the torturous conditions of a lack of food, water, and days and days of marching in the rough terrain. Ben would relate stories of his boyhood in Kentucky, to the soldiers in his regiment, as they circled around him and rested in the evenings. He would tell them "listen men, its only a matter of time, that we will be released." "America is winning the war!" He told them to look at the miserable condition Santa Ana's army was in. It was easy to see that they were retreating to Mexico City to get away from the Americans who were chasing them!

As Benjamin and his band of several hundred soldiers passed through small towns and villages along the way to Mexico City, they were shown to the local Mexicans as they were marched through the middle of town. The march took on a parade atmosphere, as they were targets of rocks, brooms and yells of "kill the Gringos!" Since Santa Ana had nothing to show for his battles with the Americans, as he lost most of them, he used the prisoners as spoils of the war, and what little success he had. As Ben could see, it was all a big show to keep the Mexicans from throwing rocks at them, since they were losing the war! As they reached the City, they could hear the people yelling for Santa Ana's army. Word had reached Mexico City a few days earlier, telling of his heroic exploits. The American prisoners were later to be mocked, cursed and in some cases beaten. It was a difficult day, as Benjamin and his fellow troops entered the city. They felt disgraced, dehumanized and pitiful, as they tried to stand tall and show they weren't beaten yet, the war wasn't over!

The parade lasted all day, as the prisoners were pushed, shoved, and splattered with garbage. It was the most humiliating time in Benjamin's life. As they were led down cobblestone streets, they could see the Bastille of sorts, with its high brick walls and fortified doors. He did not know how long he would have to be here. The interior walls and surroundings were just as fortified and filthy. The water was dirty and the food was scarce and delivered to the prisoners from outside the walls. A commanding officer called for a line up of all remaining prisoners, as many had died on the journey there. As Benjamin heard the call, he and the remaining prisoners got up and tried to overcome the pain from their legs and hips from such a long, fast march through the Mexican terrain. They were given the rules; "if you attempt to escape, you will be shot on sight!" Their meal ration for the day consisted of two cents per day. This allowed for a tortilla and some beans they could buy from a private vendor who brought food into the prison. The work assignments were filthy as they were required to clean the gutters and underground sewers. They lived in stench and vermin day and night. They came across dead bodies that were left to rot in the sewers from time to time. As they carried them out to the fields to bury, the smell would make them vomit, it was so sickening.

The food allotment was barely enough to stay alive. This gave Ben the challenge of his life, as he wanted to see his family in Kentucky again and was willing to make the best of things to continue living. By the time they began to work a daily routine, Ben had gathered a band of Kentuckians who swore to try their best to survive.

They would gather together each evening in one corner of the prison, and tell stories of their better days in Kentucky. The funny stories, like the time Ben's horse threw him into a creek after stepping in a gopher hole. As he attempted to crawl out of the shallow creek, he came face to face with a water moccasin, a poisonous snake that was ready to strike and bite him. He recalled crawling away from the snake on all fours, into a muddy area of the creek. This action saved his life, but left him muddy from head to toe. When he walked home, and knocked on the door, he was refused entry, as his appearance made them afraid to let him in. He looked like a dirty, deranged stranger. This required him to identify himself, as he begged to be let in. When the door opened, he was met with a large bucket of water being thrown at his face, to clean him up. He was then ordered to go out behind the barn and jump into the cows water tank for a bath! The tale left all his friends laughing and slapping their knees in a hilarious gesture. The stories would continue late into the dark night. Under cover of darkness you could see their eyes glisten, as the moonlight would glance off their tear filled eyes. Their emotions would sometimes turn from laughter to sobbing as they pondered their fate.

Ben would reach out and hug the sobbing soldiers, especially the young boys who hurt the most. He knew their thoughts were back home and how much they felt they had lost, by joining the army and not staying home. Each morning found them hungry, tired and depressed as they were awaken at daybreak and marched off to work. The hot sun made their days long and painful as they tried to breath the foul air, full of smoke from burning garbage. This miserable existence of theirs left them worried and wondering if they would ever be rescued. Ben's long hair and beard began to turn white from the worry of it all. The continued beatings of the troops by their captors, when they felt they weren't working hard enough, to the lack of food and medicine for their ills, left some of them contemplating suicide! This made Ben angry and determined to show the Mexicans that he was not going to give up his life in this dirty, filthy place. Each evening he continued to try and cheer up his friends with stories of happier times and words of encouragement. He would remind them that the war would soon end with their release and return to Kentucky.

The two cents a day food ration left Ben hungry as well as the rest of the troops. He noticed that the cooks, who entered the prison to sell their food, would place flat rocks on the tortillas to allow for faster cooking. This gave Ben an idea, when he went out to work each day he would look for flat rocks and finding them would stick them in his pocket, and bring them back to the prison. Each evening when the cooks began cooking, he would bargain with them, and trade his flat rocks for more tortillas. This was a successful scheme, which was passed on to his friends, allowing them to supplement their small portion of daily food.

Although Ben and his fellow prisoners were not allowed any contact with the outside world, they would write letters to their loved ones anyway, hoping that somehow they could find someone who would deliver them. Many of the troops couldn't write and would come to Ben and a few others who could, and beg them to write a letter for them. Ben knew it was good for their morale and there was the chance that those who didn't survive, could at least have one of their surviving buddies deliver it to their loved one's when the war was over. On many occasions when left unsupervised or not under observation, Ben would approach any Mexican he made contact with and pleaded with them to send a letter he would give them in secret.

To his knowledge, none of his attempts to get word to his home in Kentucky that he was still alive, ever panned out. His old Kentucky home with all his family and friends,never gave up hope that he would be released some day. They believed the war would end and he would return home.

Ben's family and wife Melvina had received the news of his capture and imprison-ment and felt that he was strong enough to survive the ordeal and return home. As the months drug on, Ben could hear chatter in the streets that the "Gringo was coming". The ships of soldiers and calvary on land, were approaching Mexico City. This meant that the war was nearing an end. Whenever possible, Ben would pass the word around, "our ships are coming, we'll be free soon!" This thought kept their spirits up as word of defeat after defeat of the Mexican army reached their ears.

It was President James K. Polk from Tennessee who started the war with Mexico and finished it, with an armada of ships and calvary sent deep into Mexico. He sent two of his best generals, Winfield Scott and Zackary Taylor to Mexico to lead the American forces to victory. It was a day Ben said "he would never forget." He and his comrades awoke to the sounds of Mexicans yelling "the Americans have landed in Vera Cruz! They are coming to Mexico City." The distant sound of cannon fire was music to their ears. The prison was eventually left unguarded as the Mexican soldiers ran to specific areas outside the city to fight off the invaders.

The war was soon over, as the Mexican Army was no match for the American armada. The amphibious invasion in 1847 landed thousands of American soldiers on Mexican soil at Vera Cruz. The following battle was over in just a few days as General Winfield Scott led his troops into Mexico City. As Ben and his fellow American prisoners left the prison, escorted by hundreds of American troops, they looked back at the rat hole that was their home for eight months. They slowly came to a stop and thanked the Lord and their country for rescuing them. They had survived one of the worst ordeals of their life, only to be thrown into another war a few years later.

The Mexican-American war brought death to 13,000 U.S. soldiers, the majority from disease rather than enemy fire. The trip back to America was on an army ship, as Ben as well as the other troops received medical attention for dysentery and other maladies. Their heads were full of lice and lack of proper hygiene left them unhealthy and weak. Ben was honorably discharged on June 7, 1847 but not released from the Army until the end of September, when he immediately went to Kentucky. The Kentucky brigade's trip back home took them from New Orleans and then by steam boat up the Mississippi to the Ohio River and then home to Kentucky and their loved ones.

As word was passed on from farm to farm that Ben and his fellow soldiers were on their way back, Ben approached his home on horseback, as kids ran ahead of him, telling everyone they saw that Ben was coming home! His long beard and head of hair had turned pure white from the ordeal. He was hardly recognizable as he got off his horse to a welcoming crowd of wife, family and friends. Thus ended a chapter in the life of Benjamin Shacklett Dowell, a true hero to many, who was later to continue his adventure into the Western frontier.

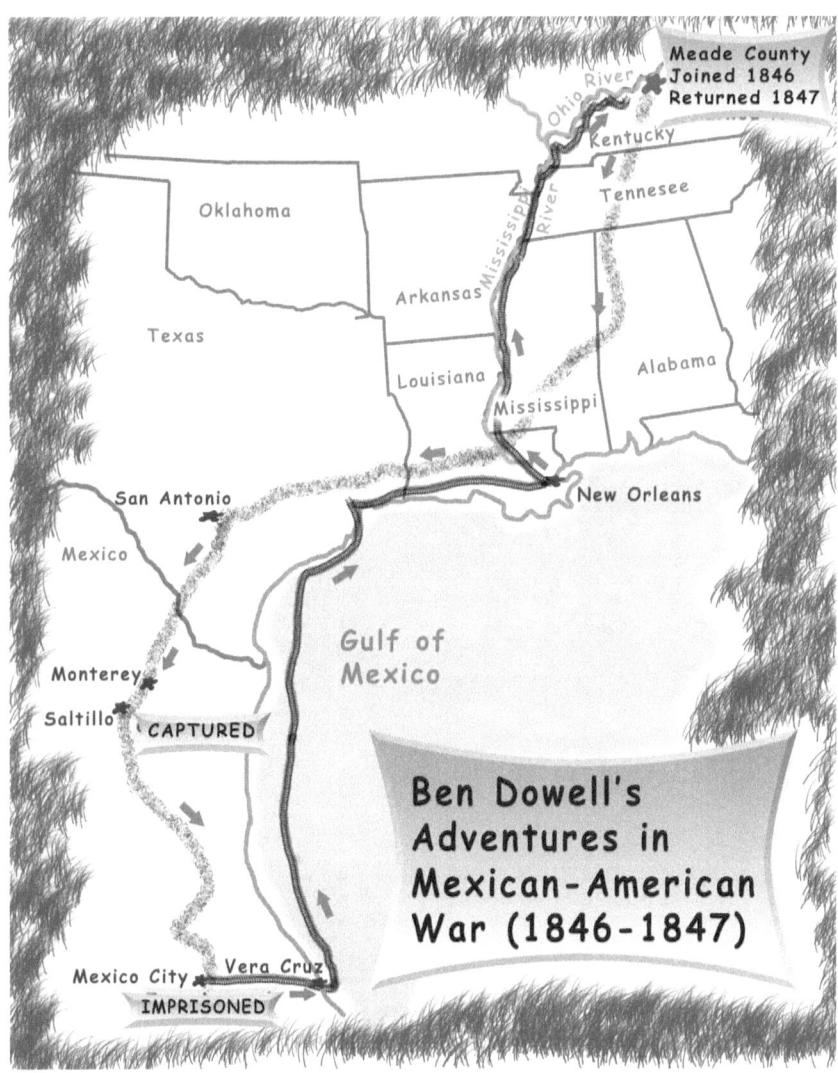

Fig.17   Routes Taken by Ben Dowell in Mexican-American War

Chapter VIII

Ben's Return to the Midwest

Although Ben's wife, Melvina and his large family were happy to see him return from the war, he began to feel restless and missed the west. His attempts to convince his wife to go West ended in their divorce, as she was unwilling to join him.

As Ben planned for the trip, he heard of a wagon train headed west that he could travel with. Even though his father and mother urged him to stay near them, Ben already had a taste of the west and there was no stopping him. He continued to prepare for his journey and after some time, said good bye again to his family and ex-wife, Melvina. He then set out on a wagon train bound for the West thru the El Paso Valley. He reached the western tip of Texas about 1850, leaving all his comforts of home. He knew he was facing many dangers with wild Indians and what he may encounter. He also felt, if he could survive a Mexican prison for eight months, he could live through anything. Ben knew he needed to find a steady income way before his money ran out. He knew that in order to fulfill his dream of succeeding, he had to utilize all the skills he learned from his parents on the farm. He had a way with animals, especially horses. He knew how to shoe them and break a horse for a saddle if need be. He also learned how to run a business as his father had taught him at a young age. His father, James Board Dowell was a horse trader and crop farmer. He taught all of his sons and daughters how to run the business. By the time Benjamin reached El Paso, the United States and Mexico had already set the boundary between the two countries by The Treaty of Guadalupe Hidalgo in 1848. The meandering "Rio Grande" was the border between the United States and Mexico.

The discovery of gold in California brought an influx of wagon trains moving West. After crossing the desert to the East of El Paso Valley, the travelers stopped at the pass for rest and supplies. In August, 1849 some 4000 emigrants with 1200 to 1500 wagons reportedly were encamped in the area. Provisions became scarce for both the people and their livestock, and the valley residents experienced a period of unusual hardship.

No one knows why Benjamin Dowell chose to stay in El Paso. He may have been among the hundreds of immigrants, stranded in the valley when wagon trains were unable to move further, and disbanded. He may have heard of the profits to be made in trading, an occupation that was beginning to attract Americans to the area. Once Benjamin decided to settle in El Paso, he began to look for work. Fortunately, he had learned to speak Spanish during his imprisonment in Mexico City. This proved to be invaluable, as there were Mexicans and Indians who spoke only Spanish in the area. The few English speaking immigrants in El Paso made up only a small percent of settlers living there at that time.

Eventually, Benjamin found work on a vineyard owned by the Ponce de Leon family. Juan Maria Ponce de Leon a wealthy trader, had a huge land holding which was given to him under land grants of 1827 and 1830. His ranching and farming interests were extensive on both sides of the Rio Grande River. It was the Ponce Ranch that was to become downtown El Paso and the site of Dowell's later business endeavors. It was here that the United States was securing its territory by sending the military to places where Mexico had formerly claimed authority in Texas, New Mexico, Arizona and California. The military post of El Paso was established September 8, 1849 using buildings on the Ponce Rancho. Troops remained there until 1851 after which the property was returned to Ponce, who held it until his death in 1852. The Ponce heirs sold the ranch for $10,000 in 1854 to a Missourian named William T. Smith. Benjamin worked on the Ponce Ranch for several years, watching it change hands several times and covering the area that is now downtown El Paso.

As Benjamin began to familiarize himself with the El Paso Valley area, he spent much time on the Tigua Indian reservation. His friendly nature and business dealings that were connected with the Ponce Ranch selling wine and brandy allowed him to meet many various Indian Tribes. The continued contact with the Tigua Indian Tribe lead to some socializing in the various Indian festivals. Benjamin met a petite, pretty Tigua Indian Princess, Juana Marquez, that he became attracted to. She belonged to a prominent Tigua family whose members included tribal "caciques", elected religious leaders. The tiny stature of Juana reminded Benjamin of his tiny mother, who was also small in stature. Juana was well trained as a homemaker and knew the etiquette of both Spanish and Indian cultures. She did not converse in English, but could understand it fairly well. She had no formal schooling and did not read or write. This made little difference to Benjamin however, who fell in love with her pretty smile and compassionate ways.

The wedding took place at Concordia, a part of the El Paso area, and a Judge Rufus Doane officiated. The date was sometime in 1852, and Benjamin was thirty four and his wife, Juana was a young nineteen. They went to live on the Ponce Ranch and Benjamin prepared a house for his lovely bride, made of adobe.

Fig.18   Paso Del Norte on Trade Route from Cerro Gordo to Santa Fe

The area known as El Paso Del Norte meant " the pass of the North"
in Spanish. This was the Northern Trade Route from Cerro Gordo,
Mexico, to Sante Fe, New Mexico. The Rio Grande River divided
this area and later became the divider between Mexico and Texas.

The Northern side of the river became known as Franklin City
in 1849. It was named after the first Postmaster General, Benjamin
Franklin Coons. This name appeared on stage time tables of the time,
confirming that it was indeed a recognized name of the place. History
revealed, however, that the name never stuck. Later, this area North of
the Rio Grande became known as El Paso, Texas, and was incorporated
on May 17, 1873. The Southern side 0f the Rio Grande River became
known as Juarez, Mexico, named after the President of Mexico.

CHAPTER IX

"THE CALL OF THE WEST"

Since Ben's work took him throughout the area of El Paso, he become acquainted with the local towns people. His likeable demeanor brought him Spanish, Indian as well as white settler friends. He became a close friend of William M. Ford, a prominent property holder. Just two years after El Paso county was organized, Ford was elected Sheriff on August 2, 1852. He appointed Benjamin as Deputy, administering the oath of office on March 21, 1853. By the virtue of these offices, the two became involved in a skirmish in Dona Ana County, New Mexico in January 1854. James Magoffin, a land owner in El Paso, obtained the rights to a salt deposit in Dona Ana County on the east slope of the San Andres Mountains. When he learned that salt was being stolen by persons living in New Mexico, he organized a posse of twenty eight men from El Paso including Benjamin and his friend, Ford.

The posse set out to stop the thieves. They were armed with a Howitzer which proved to be too much for the one hundred twenty five New Mexicans at their point of encounter. The possession and use of a Howitzer was illegal, therefore prosecutable by law. While Benjamin and his friend Ford were not named in indictments by the United States

District Courts of New Mexico, the trouble inspired them to leave town and seek gold in California.

They packed up their families and followed the Gila Trail through Southern New Mexico and Arizona. The Gadsden Treaty had set the border between Mexico and the United States along there as recently as December 30, 1853. Like other travelers fearful of the Indians, they joined a wagon train.

Benjamin Dowell and his friend William Ford had seen many fortune seekers pass through El Paso going West, most of them spurred by the 1848 discovery along the American River in California. The two did not go North to the gold fields however, but stopped in Los Angeles. In 1850, Los Angeles was a town of about 1600 people, but mushroomed to 4400 by 1860. During this growth period, corruption reigned and many considered it the wickedest city on the continent.

Fights, murders, lynchings, and robberies were daily occurrences. Newspapers of the time published a California Homicide Calendar with box scores for killings, hangings by the Sheriff and hangings by the mobs. Although Benjamin and Ford were in unfamiliar surroundings that brought them daily fear, they soon discovered that an immediate need of the people flocking to Los Angeles was housing. They became carpenters and earned a respectable living, in contrast with those who expected to get rich quick at gold prospecting. Benjamin Dowell was heard saying "I saw more broke people than people with gold!"

As Benjamin and Ford began to earn a respectable living through their carpentry business, they felt that they were on their way to prosperity. Yet, they both missed the El Paso area and never felt safe and comfortable in Los Angeles.

The news from Benjamin's wife Juana that she was carrying a child was the final determining factor in his decision to return to El Paso and a more safe place to bring up his child. He strongly felt that Los Angeles was not a fit place for her.

After the birth of their first child, Mary, on October 31, 1854, they began to plan their return to Texas. Before they left, however, Benjamin took his daughter to the seashore and washed her face in the water of the Pacific. "This" he told her, "is so when you are grown up, you can say," 'I cannot remember the land of my birth, but my face was washed in the ocean water there.'

Although Benjamin was a matter-of-fact kind of person, he still displayed a lovable, philosophical view of life with people around him. When Mary was six months old and strong enough to make the trip back to El Paso, the Dowell's and Ford's joined a wagon train for the trip back. It was long and arduous as there were many fierce Indian Tribes along the way that looked for a chance to attack anyone who strayed away from the wagon train. The trip went well, however, except for one incident that put fear in Benjamin and Juana. One night, the wagon train stopped and camped at Cooke's Springs, a few miles East of the present Arizona State line in southern New Mexico. Juana Dowell prepared a pallet on the side of the wagon and laid the baby there early in the morning while the adults ate breakfast. A coyote came into the camp and snatched the baby by her clothing, running away with her. Benjamin heard the baby cry and with a cool head that the he was noted for, picked up a gun and fired at the coyote, killing it. Juana ran to the baby and scooped her up, unhurt but a little frightened. Benjamin's quick action saved his daughter.

Upon their return to El Paso, they noticed it was beginning to take on new life, partly due to the continuing influx of travelers moving West, and also due to a new interest by the military.

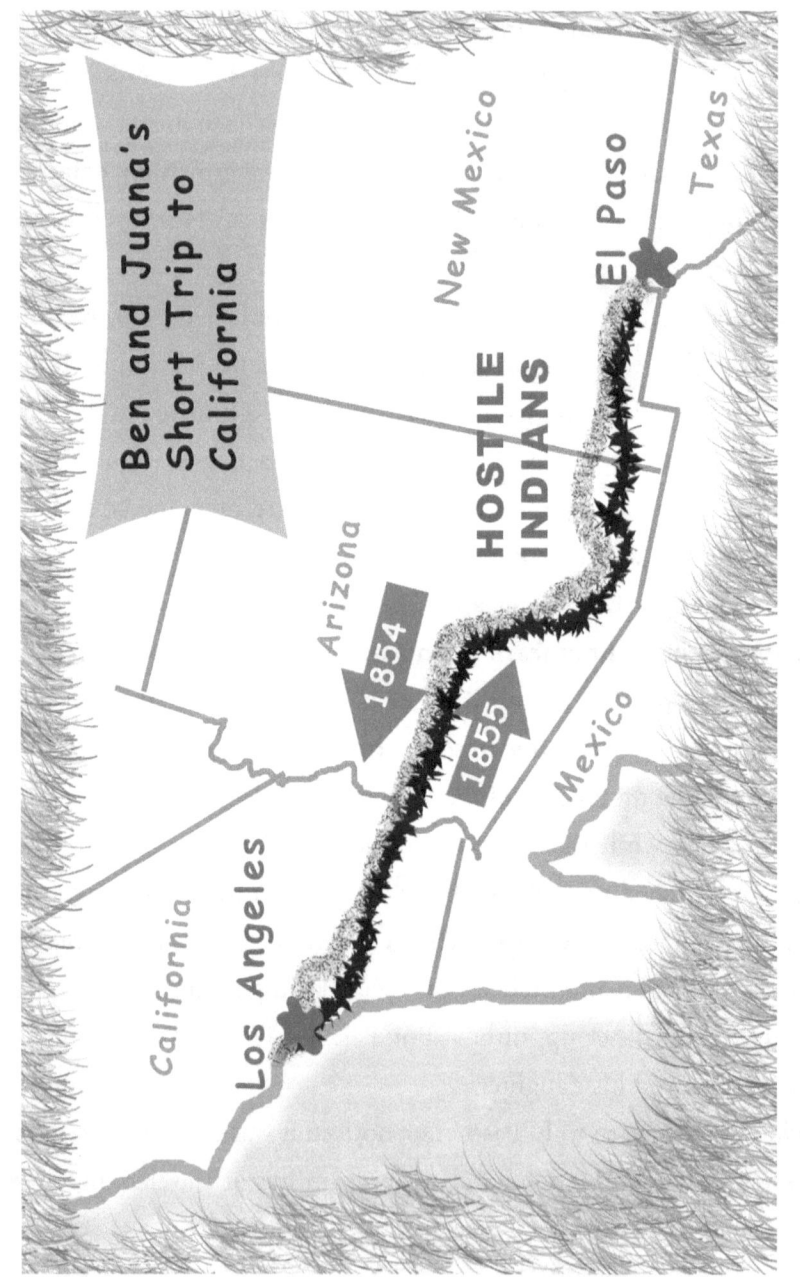

Fig. 19   Ben and Juana's Trip to California (1854 - 1855)

CHAPTER X

PRE-CIVIL WAR YEARS

Upon Ben's and William's return, Benjamin found the Ponce Ranch being managed by a close friend of his, William T. (Uncle Billy) Smith. Out of friendship and respect, "Uncle Billy" turned the management of the ranch over to Benjamin, and he continued to run it until it was partitioned into a town by Anson Mills first survey and plat in 1859. Benjamin began to learn the business of wine and brandy making and he noticed that there were many passing travelers and military men who stopped by the vineyard for wine and brandy on a regular basis. Their wine and brandies were said to be the best in the area, by passing travelers. Since Benjamin had a sharp eye for business ventures, he saw the need for a saloon in El Paso, since there weren't any. He opened his saloon on Alameda Street (currently El Paso Street in downtown El Paso). This was El Paso's first saloon and grew to be known as the Monte Carlo of the West due to all the gambling done there. Being a saloon keeper was no disgrace in those days. In fact, it was used for town hall meetings to discuss official business.

Among the distinctions of Benjamin's saloon was that it became the town's first official Post Office. This led to him being one of the first Postmasters of El Paso, holding the job from March 6, 1857 to

September 15, 1860. The mail was carried by horseback in those days and the local citizens became irate when they were losing mail carriers who were being attacked and killed by the Indians. At a citizens meeting in Benjamin's saloon on April 1, 1858, they discussed the lack of protection by the military.

This prompted Benjamin to write a letter to the Postmaster General, Aaron V. Brown, contending that the government was not doing its part to protect the mail carriers from Indian attacks and he wanted help from soldiers in the area. The reply came from the Capital stating; "you are authorized by the honorable Secretary of War, James B. Floyd by order of the President of the United States, James Buchanan, to appear to the Commanders of Fort Bliss and Fort Filmore, for a sufficient guard of soldiers to guarantee the protection of the mails from the attacks of wild Indians which infest the region." This accommodation was made noting that the mail had increased over 100percent, that is from four letters to ten letters twice each week.

The opportunity for Benjamin to succeed in business around town grew at a fast pace, as he was fair minded, helpful to others and a pillar in the community.

Besides operating the Post Office and his saloon/store, he ran a hotel and operated the Stagecoach stand, caring for the horses and performing other duties. He provided services for the stage line by boarding horses, and supplying relay services. As though this was not enough to keep Benjamin busy, he bought a ranch eight miles up the Rio Grande Valley from El Paso where he raised the beef he butchered to supply the Army Post on a contract basis.

Through Benjamin's experience as a carpenter in the early days when he was in Los Angeles, California, he knew the value of wood for building and would deliver it from his ranch to town on twelve burros he used for delivery. The side business from cattle allowed him to start a small dairy and deliver fresh milk by mule from his ranch every morning to be sold in town. During this time, there were many men looking for jobs and many needed services for the influx of travelers through El Paso, as well as settlers, Benjamin was always quick to see a chance to start a new business.

During the years Benjamin and his friend, Ford, were in California, the Masons began to group as a powerful community source. They built the El Paso Lodge No 130 in 1854. The Ancient Free and Accepted Masons, was just a year old when Benjamin returned from California in May of 1855. It had been Chartered January 24, 1854. The lodge was instituted on April 8, 1854 with eleven charter members in a ceremony in the Grand Central Hotel. Benjamin became active in this group because he wanted to be a part of the growth in El Paso. As a member he helped make major decisions concerning El Paso. He received his Master Mason's degree at a meeting before the Civil War on April 7, 1859. Among those present, were his brother Nim, who belonged to Big Springs, Kentucky Lodge No. 118. The members scattered during the Civil War years, of 1861-1865. Work was resumed on July 8, 1866. The eight men present included four pre-war members including Ben Dowell. At the election of December 5, 1868, Benjamin was named the lodges' sixth Worshipful Master, being installed March 6, 1869.

Benjamin's ability to solve problems and handle delicate situations, made him a worthy member. The Masonic Lodge did many important things to promote the general welfare of the community. On September 5, 1874, Benjamin was authorized by the lodge to bid on land to be used as a Masonic Cemetery. The land was purchased for forty dollars, and remained a cemetery until 1885, when it was moved to its present location at Concordia Street in El Paso. In 1878, he was also instrumental in obtaining a new lodge in downtown El Paso. He had been appointed District Deputy Grand Master in early 1870, and continued in that office until his death in 1880. By 1875, there were three chartered lodges in Ben Dowell's district.

The years of working for a better El Paso paid off as Benjamin became more prominent and a well known citizen. El Paso's settlers decided one day that their town was destined for a great future. They began to organize a government to cope with some of their problems. The railroads were inching their way toward the pass, not to arrive until 1881, but already influencing those who looked ahead. An 1872 census counted 764 residents. The Texas Legislature incorporated the city of El Paso on May 17, 1873. Benjamin began to inform his constituents and citizenry that big things were about to happen to El Paso. The railroad was approaching, bringing with it many new residents and growth.

Fig. 20   Fort Bliss (1854)

Fig. 21   Butterfield Stage Station (1858)

Chapter XI

Shoot-Out at Benjamin's Saloon

Benjamin's business ventures began to blossom, along with success came some troubles and problems. Benjamin was overheard to say "it wasn't long before I found out that keeping a saloon was a mixed job. It didn't only mean selling drinks and cigars and running gambling games, it meant keeping out of trouble by not playing any favorites in little fusses, and keeping little fusses out of the saloon. It was also necessary to keep an eye on the bad men who wanted to start trouble. "There were times it wasn't easy, but I kept my mouth shut most of the time, and didn't have but mighty little trouble." Yet, with all the manipulating Benjamin did to keep trouble out of his saloon, it found him and involved him whether he liked it or not. If he had been the type to notch his gun for killings, he could have cut a few grooves. He had a steady eye, and his goatee, his daughter Mary called cornstalks, as well as his prematurely gray hair, lent him an air of authority. He became known around town as "Uncle Ben" a friendly, helpful sort of guy who was always trying to patch up trouble and go by the "live and let live" policy.

In the fall of 1855, Benjamin was awakened in the night by the loud barks from his dogs. He quickly got out of bed and looked in his corral and discovered that all the horses were gone except one. His suspicion centered on two men known as William Gifford and William McElroy who had fled after breaking into the saloon taking three guns and other articles. McElroy had a bad reputation for killing two men in California.

Their escape route had been North toward Las Cruces, New Mexico. There was a robbery of the Custom's house safe at about the same time with a loss of $2,300, part of which was government funds and the rest belonged to various individuals. It was noted that McElroy and a few of his friends were also involved in this robbery as well.

Benjamin and his friends were able to track down and recapture his livestock except for two prize horses. Eight months later, McElroy heard that Benjamin had been telling people that he was responsible for the theft and wanted to settle accounts with him, especially for stealing his livestock. When McElroy heard this, he began to make threats on Benjamin's life. Coming in from Indian Country on August 6, 1856, McElroy and his friend Gordon, headed for the small town of San Elizario to spend the night. They sought refreshment in William Fords bar, unaware that he was a close friend of Benjamin's.

As liquor loosened their tongues, Ford picked up the information that they planned to go to Benjamin's saloon early the next morning. They plotted that one would go inside and ask for a drink, while the other waited outside. When Benjamin turned his back to get the liquor, he would be shot and robbed. William Ford played along with the would be killers, until he got all the information he needed. William wrote a note about the plot and had a fast rider carry it to Benjamin. When the saloon-grocery store opened the next morning, a few well armed friends were hidden behind the cracker barrels. Then, right on schedule, the robbers showed up. When McElroy entered the door, Benjamin nailed him with a well-armed shot. McElroy stumbled and turned and then was shot by a bullet through the head, fired by Benjamin's friend Albert Kuhn. A news report of the gun fight noted that the end of the West's worst criminal and bank robber came to an end. The death of McElroy later revealed that he was also involved in the Custom House robbery in El Paso. His demise left the country side safer and more peaceful, for a while anyway.

The saloon, as the town's most popular gathering place, was the site of many other shooting incidents totally unrelated to Benjamin. The fatal shooting of Dallas Stoudenmier, a Marshall who had vowed to clean up El Paso, took place in Benjamin's bar. It was part of the growing pains El Paso went through in its attempts to tame the wild west. When physical fights broke out in the saloon, it was customary to just let them go, unrestrained as long as guns weren't involved. A friend of Benjamin's by the name of W. W. Mills arrived in El Paso in 1858 and learned a lesson in local etiquette. When a fight broke out in the saloon between two customers, he tried to stop the melee and was told by Benjamin "my young friend, when you see anything of that kind going on in El Paso, don't interfere. It is not considered good manners here!"

Many people were shot and killed in Benjamin's saloon. On March 23, 1858 a gambler named Tom Smith shot and killed a doctor by the name of Frank Giddings. Giddings had lived in El Paso four years before being shot. Tom Smith fled to Mexico and was never heard from again. W. W. Mills had witnessed another "accidental" death when he saw an innocent bystander killed in the post office. (As this was his account of the incident, he called it the post office but was actually the saloon.) A gambler had aimed at another gambler and missed, hitting and killing the bystander.

The coroner's jury ruled it purely accidental, extending abundant sympathy to the unfortunate man who's aim had been so poor, as to miss his mark. Nobody paid much attention to the victim.

Benjamin witnessed a gunslinger taking a shot at the popular legislator, Jeff Hall, on the main street in front of the saloon. A dozen or more upset and angry citizens started after the gunman, cornering him in what was known as Hell's Half Acre, the corral in back of the Central hotel. The shootout involved several gunshots that brought down the gunslinger. The citizens began arguing over who actually killed him. Benjamin reminded them that a judge could ride into town seeking an investigation as to who killed the gunslinger. This immediately stopped the boasting. The fastest coroner's jury ever held in El Paso convened and ruled that the deceased "came to his death by gunshot wounds from hands of parties unknown." Benjamin's actual words to the citizenry as recorded was "Gentlemen, some day some judge or other may come along and be holding court, and some of us may have trouble about this business."

In an incident which occurred in 1875 according to a Mormon Missionary visiting at the time, an outlaw gang attempted to take over the town. They came into town with guns blazing and tried to take over the saloon. Benjamin was acting as Marshall at the time, and Daniel W. Jones had succeeded him as Mayor. When the gang was relaxing in the saloon and let their guard down, Benjamin and the Mayor put together a posse and managed to arrest the men after a gun battle that left some citizenry dead. The posse managed to arrest the men with Benjamin and the Mayor's help. Benjamin, the judge, the mayor, and others delegated to the task, shot four of the condemned men on the street in front of the saloon and the men were duly buried. So, ended the attempted take over of El Paso by a ruthless gang of men. The Mormon Missionary said he was shown the court records and never heard any complaint about the proceedings, but on the other hand, Judge Jones and Benjamin S. Dowell were very much respected by the average citizen of El Paso for what they did.

As far as the violent shoot-outs in El Paso went, Benjamin was not involved in most of them, except in defense. He had a reputation for trying to head off the fireworks when possible, but he accepted the fact that some men just had to settle things with guns in early El Paso.

Back

Front

Fig. 22   Dowell Saloon Chips Made from U.S. Quarters

Ben Dowell's Business Seen from Overland Building

Fig. 23   Ben Dowell's Business about the Time he Died   (1880)

Ben Dowell's Business at El Paso & Overland Streets

Fig. 24   El Paso Street (1880) Showing Ben Dowell's Business at End

Chapter XII

A Trip Home to Kentucky

In 1860, things were going well for Benjamin and his family. His businesses were growing and making him well known in the El Paso area as a prominent citizen.

He felt comfortable with those who worked for him and didn't need to overlook his holdings as close as he once did. He longed to see his parents, brothers and sisters in the lush country along the Ohio River in Kentucky. He wanted his wife Juana and daughter Mary, to see Kentucky and meet his relatives. He hadn't been back since just after the Mexican American War.

Before he left, he authorized his brother, Nim, who had been living in El Paso for some time, to handle his affairs if he should die during the trip. Since Benjamin wanted his family to be safe from wild Indians, he planned his trip well, with large groups of people who banded together to remain safe as they moved through the countryside. The first part of his trip was with a mule train belonging to Alexandre Daguerre, who was taking his small son to school in San Antonio, Texas. Daguerre was a prominent operator of wagon trains in the area and his family, who lived in Paso Del Norte, had been long close friends of the Dowell's. Ben purchased what was called an ambulance wagon which was closed on all sides and contained a large bed. It was driven by a man called Queen, who was familiar with the trail to Galveston, Texas. Ben had also purchased a wagon for groceries and other supplies and paid a French cook to go along and prepare the meals.

As they neared San Antonio, they camped in Kinney County, West of town and spent three days there at Turkey Creek. The place was well named as there were many wild turkeys in the woods surrounding the area. Benjamin took the opportunity to hunt wild turkeys with his friends on the trail and killed their share, before they left for San Antonio. Upon reaching San Antonio, they took the time to look up an old friend of Benjamin's by the name of Mr. Woldrick, where they stayed several days talking old times. The friendship grew, from trips Benjamin had made through this area on many occasions. Since they were in friendlier areas, Benjamin chose to take a stagecoach rather than a wagon train to Houston, Texas. This would be much faster and less trouble. Upon reaching Houston, they took the only railway in Texas at the time, to the gulf to Galveston. Just as they were feeling safe and secure an incident occurred which they narrowly escaped from. Benjamin hired a hack to take them from the railroad station to the hotel and the coach collided with another and over turned. The hotel owner who was riding with them and the coach driver were killed, as they sat on top of the wagon. Although Benjamin, Juana and Mary were shook up, the fact that they were riding inside the coach saved them from any harm.

The following day found them boarding a steamboat in New Orleans called the Natchez and heading up the Mississippi River. This in turn led to the Ohio River which they took to Meade County, Kentucky, their final destination. The trip was long and hard, but the joy of being home again in Kentucky, left them happy to see everyone.

Benjamin commented that every where they looked, there were Dowell's. It seemed that everyone in that part of Kentucky was related to the Dowell's. They rode horseback from one home to another, being entertained overnight and served huge meals. Benjamin carried Mary his daughter, in the saddle with him from place to place. The visits were enjoyable for Benjamin, and he was able to entertain his relatives with stories of life out west, where it was not unusual to see a man shot dead in his tracks as he walked down a street. However, for his wife Juana, it became increasingly difficult as she couldn't speak English very well. Her lack of ability to communicate with those around her, coupled with the stares and words of her being an Indian from the West, was more than she could take. She retreated to her room, where she took her meals and escaped the Kentucky stares and whispered remarks. Her inability to converse in this setting was uncomfortable and upsetting to her. The fact that Benjamin's divorced wife still lived in the neighborhood didn't help the situation either. Her name was Melvina Stith and out of curiosity wanted to talk to Benjamin, but out of respect for his wife Juana, he refused to see her.

After a month of relaxation and visiting family and friends, Benjamin felt it was time to head on back to his beloved El Paso. His mother and father thoroughly enjoyed their visit, especially with their granddaughter, Mary. Benjamin began to tell the same stories over and over about his adventures in the wild west and felt that he had said all there was to say, so it was time to go home and check on all his businesses. The trip to Kentucky proved timely however, as Ben's father passed away the following October 20th. Ben and Juana and Mary were grateful to have had the chance to visit with him.

The many family and friends visited by Benjamin and his family, while in Kentucky, were amazed and excited over the success of his ventures and stories of the West. Benjamin had invited many of them to accompany him as their guests back to El Paso. His sister, Susan Jane Dowell Shacklett, her husband, Burnis B. Shacklett and their four children chose to return with Benjamin to live in El Paso. One of their children, Barbara, who was two years old, was a year younger than Mary at the time. The trip back was written in a diary which described the journey in some detail.

The travelers took a boat in April, 1860 called the Montgomery, down the Ohio River from Rock Haven, Kentucky. As they neared Paducah, Kentucky, a storm damaged their boat and they had a few days lay over until the repairs could be made.

Once they were able to proceed, they made it into New Orleans, stopping there two days and two nights. The journey continued as they crossed the river and took a train to the bay. There they boarded a ship for Port Lavaca. The ship took them to Galveston after two days travel, and then on to Port Lavaca. There they waited for several days to have their goods unloaded. Once unloaded, they hitched to Benjamin's waiting wagons and started out by land to El Paso. Their trip would take them 800 miles through San Antonio, Texas. The weary travelers reached San Antonio, exhausted and suffering from the hot weather and mosquitoes. They decided to rest up while there and camp out for a week.

After a three hundred mile trip west on Turkey Creek, their fears of wild Indians forced them to wait a full month for a wagon train to travel with. The following travel over the plains was extremely difficult due to washed out trails and tremendous heat.

Most of their journey was at night, as the Indians were so fierce and attacked settlers who were traveling alone. The trail was also scarce of water and they could never carry enough to last them. The distance between watering holes was about forty miles apart, making it difficult to water the animals. As they reached each watering place, they would stop to rest and cook something to eat until another stop.

After a long and tiring journey, they reached El Paso on August 18, 1860. Benjamin and all the family were so happy to be home. His holdings and businesses survived without him, as he had good and trusted men to watch out for him, especially his brother, Nim. Benjamin's sister, Susan Shacklett was one of three Anglo women living in town at the time and she was the first to churn butter and sell it in El Paso, asking $1.00 per pound. Unfortunately, Indian raids were common in those days and Susan's milkman who took her butter and buttermilk to town for sale was killed. The Shacklett family lived on a ranch up the river from the village. The milkman would carry milk on burros in two large cans tied on each side. The ranchers in the area had high walls around their house lots, and stables, to protect them against Indian raiders, but the Indians would shoot their arrows straight up and over the walls, often killing a milk cow or a fine horse. Susan Shacklett knew a stage coach driver who would stop at the ranch to treat himself and his passengers to her buttermilk. One day when he stopped, he told her, "this drink will probably be my last, as I am sure the Indians will get me this trip!" His premonitions were correct. He was shot off the coach and his passengers all were scalped.

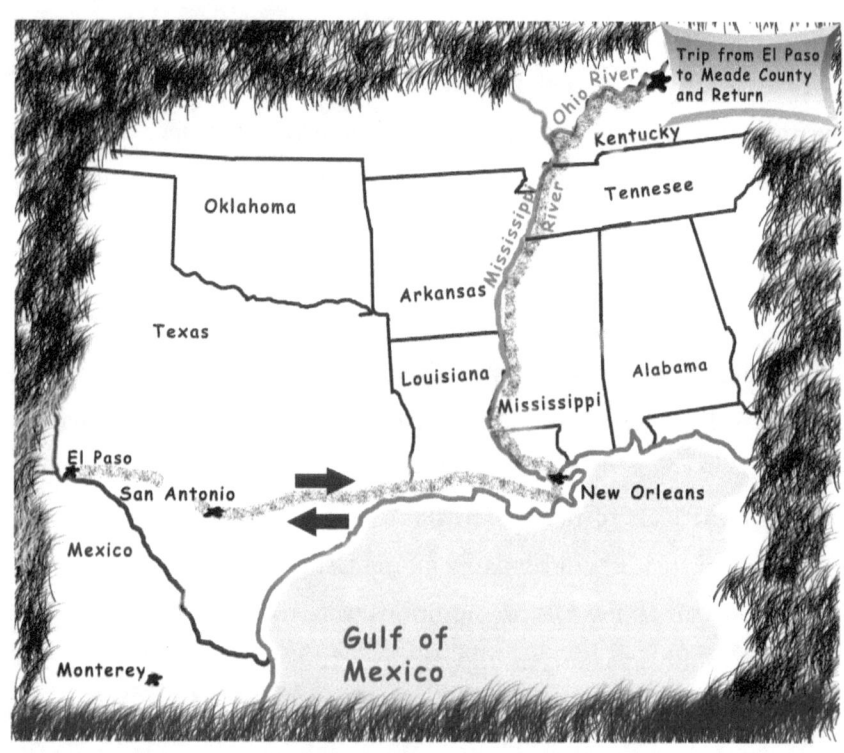

Fig. 25 Ben and Juana's Trip to Meade County, Kentucky, and Back

Fig. 26   Bernice B. Shacklett and Susan Dowell Shacklett

Chapter XIII

A War Is Coming

It was in the early 1860's when things were just beginning to improve economically for everyone. Benjamin was becoming a prominent, wealthy citizen of El Paso. His saloon was booming with customers and his farm as well as other side businesses were highly successful. When he thought all was well with the world, a whisper, then a shout of war began to fill the street. Everyday brought more news of a Civil War between the states. It was scary to be sure. By then he had his family and businesses to worry about. How would he protect them with fighting all around?

The border states, as they were called; Kentucky, Tennessee, and surrounding states were sympathetic to the South. The Confederacy had his allegiance, since the South was his culture and way of life. It now was being threatened by the very country that was suppose to protect them. When Benjamin received letters from home, of the pending war, he wished he could be there to protect his mother and family in Kentucky. He knew however, his hands would be full as the war reached them. The many angry, boisterous people entering the saloon, only made Benjamin feel more patriotic for the Confederacy, as Texas was all for the South. In a display of patriotism, Benjamin was the first person in El Paso to fly a Confederate flag. He climbed to the top of his hotel and planted a Southern flag. As he did, many friends cried out "you'll be killed", but Benjamin wouldn't let this stop him, even though it was a dangerous political statement to make. El Paso's vote showed a unanimous support of the South with a total vote of over 800. This was interesting since there were only suppose to be 428 citizens in the City of El Paso at the time. Apparently many Mexicans from across the river came to vote.

Benjamin decorated up his saloon with many southern flags and since it was the most popular place in town, turned it into a voting place for the secession election. The political feelings ran so deep in Benjamin's thoughts about saving the south that he let it effect his job as Postmaster. A prominent citizen named Anson Mills was receiving abolitionist literature about freeing the slaves from his friends back east. He claimed that Benjamin not only refused to deliver the mail after opening it, but formed a committee to burn it publicly.

Benjamin was against a war being fought, but he was drawn up into the patriotism of the day for the south. Everything he began to do was directed at helping the South prepare for the war which was inevitable. The call for war had an appeal of its own, it grew without anyone having any power to stop it. As tensions grew for succession by several states, Benjamin got news that South Carolina, Florida, Alabama, Mississippi, Louisiana, Georgia, and Texas voted to dissolve their ties with the United States. This took place in Montgomery, Alabama on February 4, 1861. They formed a new nation called The Confederate States of America. They picked Jefferson Davis as their President who was from Mississippi.

The first shots of the Civil War were fired on Fort Sumter, a Union Fort, by an Alabama Confederate General demanding them to surrender. The actual war between the North and South began to explode in 1861. As Texas came under the Confederacy, Fort Bliss was ordered to surrender to the Confederates, on March 31, 1861. Five companies of the Texas 2nd Mounted Rifles and a battery of the 2nd Texas Light Artillery took over. They moved into New Mexico as well, but in 1862, Brig. General Henry H. Sibley failed to take New Mexico for the Confederacy. In May, his men, their supplies cut off, made their way back to Fort Bliss after having suffered a fifty percent loss in dead, wounded, and sick prisoners of war.

As the war intensified, Benjamin's, as well as many other businesses, suffered great losses as the Confederacy took over. Benjamin began to aid the Confederacy with supplies and also joined their forces. As things got increasingly worse, Benjamin began to see the hazards of war. The maimed and crippled soldiers began to pour into El Paso. Their faces and mangled bodies told the story of just how bad things were. Benjamin came upon a small battlefield near El Paso and saw the horror of war first-hand. Bodies of Northern and Southern troops lying all over the ground. Some were crying out for help as they lay dying, bleeding to death! He did all he could to help, but it was too late for most, and graves were dug at the sight for the bodies. His passion for the war began to dwindle as he saw the suffering on both sides. He began to worry about his family as the Union troops began to reach El Paso.

Benjamin did all he could for the Confederate soldiers by providing meat and supplies. He could see the battle being lost as more and more Union soldiers entered El Paso. The families of Southern sympathizers left the area as the tide began to turn.

Some went to San Antonio and others as far as St Louis, Missouri. During the fierce battles surrounding El Paso, it became a war of cat and mouse for many families. One day they would play to the sympathies of the South, the next to the North, whoever was winning at the time.

Many times, Benjamin saw the war as a useless way of destroying everything he cared for. His allegiance began to concern itself with his family more than anything else. This became a concern when he heard that his wife, Juana was pregnant again. He quickly sent them to nearby Ysleta to be with her relatives while he remained in El Paso. He knew she would be safe there and this was where their second child, John R (Juan) was born on August 12, 1862.

As the stench of death began to fill the air around El Paso, with several skirmishes everywhere, Benjamin began to realize that the war could go on for several years even though it began to make no sense. His best friend's families began to receive death notices from the Texas volunteer Calvary who were fighting in the midst of the large battles of the South. There was also the Texas Infantry Brigade, Texas Calvary Regiment and the Texas Mounted Rifles. As the death toll increased day by day, the sound of distant explosions from the large howitzers could be heard. Benjamin knew it was only a matter of time that his beloved El Paso would be overrun with Union soldiers.

In September, 1862 Benjamin arranged for the only safe place he could think of for his family; Juana, Mary and Juan (who he named after his friend Juan Ruiz) was to take them across the river to Mexico. Juan Ruiz shared a house, duplex style with Benjamin's family. Benjamin's sister, Susan Shacklett moved her family to the small town of Sherman some distance from El Paso. Her husband was a soldier fighting in the South, leaving her alone to take care of her large family. After Benjamin insured the safety of his family, he went back to El Paso to help other Confederate sympathizers in a resistance effort.

On November, 1862, Union troops moved into El Paso. All was deathly quiet for the moment, many had left town and left most of their belongings. There were rumors of Southern sympathizers being hung and beaten. The remaining citizens of El Paso remained in their homes, hoping and praying for peace.

Benjamin, like many of his friends and citizens of El Paso, remained stubborn and adamant in their efforts to help the Confederacy. On December 12, 1862 a group met in Benjamin's home in Mexico just across the river. As he held his four month old son in his arms and paced the floor in silence, he listened to the others on ways to use the Tigua Indians to spy on Union troop movement around El Paso. He agreed with the group of well wishers for the South, and hired two Tigua Indians, Simon and Bernardo Olguin to follow a Union scouting party led by Captain N. J. Pishon, in order to spy on them. The Olguin's were related to Juana, Benjamin's wife. The spying helped the Confederate troops who were in the area, but Benjamin began to feel that he was not helpful enough for his cause. He had heard that a blockade of Galveston left the Southern soldiers lacking in clothing and uniforms. He joined the Confederate Army and attempted to run the Galveston blockade with a large shipment of cotton bound for the South. The annals of the Civil War documented the incident of the "Terista" carrying 298 bales of cotton being captured by the U.S.S. Granite near the mouth of the Rio Grande River on November 14, 1862. Benjamin escaped, unhurt in this incident. As the war carried on, Benjamin became involved as a recruiting officer with the rank of Captain.

CHAPTER XIV

A RETURN HOME TO MORE TRAGEDIES

Although Benjamin had done all he could to help the Confederacy cause, he began to realize that they were losing. His efforts had taken him far from home and his family. In July of 1863 Benjamin received news that his brother, James who had moved to El Paso years before and recently moved to Sherman, a small town outside of El Paso was dying. He had been kicked in the stomach by one of his own horses. Once Benjamin reported this to his commanding officer, he was allowed to leave to see his brother. The trip on horseback took him several days, but he was able to reach Sherman just before his brother James past away. After visiting with his sister, Susan Dowell Shacklett, who also lived in Sherman with her family, Benjamin began to get homesick. He was close to his beloved wife and children and began to change his plans of returning to duty.

As he prepared to head for Mexico just across the Rio Grande to his wife, he was given a beautiful horse by the name of Kit that his deceased brother had owned. This beautiful race horse was to inspire an important chapter in El Paso racing history. Upon leaving Sherman, he rode on his new horse Kit and pulled a pack mule along. After a few days ride, he reached the Presidio Del Norte in Mexico and spent some time with his friend John W. Burgess. Burgess had been one of the first men to arrive at the Presidio. Like Benjamin, he was also a southern sympathizer. He had tried early in the war to take a train of twenty two wagons and 220 mules to New Mexico to help the war effort there and had been captured by Union soldiers. He and one of his men managed to escape, by the time he had reached the Presidio they were starving. Now he felt it was his turn to help a fellow Confederate who was returning home.

As Benjamin and Burgess talked over their recent adventures, they were unaware that a small skirmish was taking place near the Presidio. Late that night they heard someone banging on the door of Burgess's house. They were awaken around midnight by Benjamin's old friend, William Ford, who he had gone to California with several years before. He was standing at the door clad only in his underwear. He related a story of his narrow escape from Union troops who attacked them at night. He stated that if he had taken time to dress, they would have taken him prisoner.

When it came time to move on, Ford joined Benjamin in the ride through Paso Del Norte, Texas across the Rio Grande to Chihuahua and then back north to his family. The long trip around El Paso was to ensure that they wouldn't be seen by the Union troops who were camped in the area. His eyes began to show emotion as he saw the small shack type house just over a hill where his wife Juana, his daughter Mary and his son Juan were waiting. He had been gone for a year and five months. His children had grown some and his wife Juana although happy to see him, had a look of desperation on her face as they had gone through some tough times. In order to survive, Juana had to sell the bar furniture to a friend who also lived in Paso Del Norte. The furniture had been brought with them, so they could store it and save it for their return to El Paso some day. A friend by the name of Doane used the furniture, billiard tables and other saloon fixtures to start his own small bar. His customers were Union soldiers who came across the river to Mexico, to rest and get away from the war. It was a form of R and R (rest and recuperation) for them. They paid in greenback Confederate and Union money, which in Mexico were only worth thirty cents to a dollar. Costs were high for exiled American's living in Mexico. A box of matches or a spool of thread was twenty five cents and other prices were exorbitant.

Juana began to tell Benjamin of other things she sold, in order to survive. Their household goods and even her cooking stove, as well as her fine dresses she used to wear to special occasions when things were better in El Paso. As tears filled her eyes, she continued to let Benjamin know how bad things had been and how sorry she was to have lost all of their prized possessions. Benjamin began to console her as he hugged and kissed her and assured her that after what he had seen in the war torn country of America, they were truly lucky to be alive and well. He told Juana that they would sell some jewelry and his watch and gold chain, whatever it took to survive. He let her know that it could all be replaced some day when they were on top again. He also had some property in Paso Del Norte that was rugged terrain but could be exchanged for the rent of a house and the land and fruit on it for a couple of years. Although they were experiencing tough economic times, so was everyone else. Things were particularly bad in Mexico, as they were at war with France and going through similar problems as America was.

As they were living in El Paso Del Norte, Mexico, Benjamin came home one day and told Juana that a German merchant visiting Mexico told him that the Mexican government was going to seize all the food and dole it out, according to family size.

Since they had a cow, they were assured of milk, but they had to buy bread from the government dole. Their household was five as his sister, Susan Shacklett and her family had brought a young black girl who was an orphan in Kentucky with them to El Paso.

When her husband Bernice went to war, leaving her alone with all the children to care for, she was unable to take care of the young girl. Benjamin and Juana took responsibility of her care, to help her out. Since there were five in their family, Benjamin could get five loaves of bread a day which in reality were so small they would make one ordinary sized loaf of bread.

That winter, they planted wheat, corn and other vegetables as well as tobacco. A food shortage began to occur in the spring of 1865 before the crops were ready to harvest. As the wheat ripened, the families ground the heads after drying them in the sun. Then the chaff was removed with rocks to grind it and prepare it. The green grain was ground in a small hand mill and Juana made bread from the flour that was produced. Some people were so hard up and at the brink of starving that when they got corn for planting, they would eat it instead. As the crops matured, the depression and starvation began to pass.

The number of exiled American's in Mexico reached over 10,000 before the war came to an end. This included many Confederate Officers who saw this as a way of saving themselves and their families. Then as quietly as the war began, Benjamin and all the exiled American's around them heard the news; "the war was over!" On April 9, 1865 Robert E. Lee surrendered to the Union, bringing an end to a war that had claimed more than 620,000 lives in almost five years of fierce fighting between the North and the South. The staggering death toll was part of 2.5 million men who fought for the Union and one million who fought for the Confederacy. General William T. Sherman's march to the sea through Georgia and the Carolina's, which destroyed homes and farms, left thousands of people starving and struck with terror.

The era following the Civil War from 1865-1877 was called the "reconstruction"period. Literally millions were left homeless, starving and without any idea of what they would do to survive. The government began to institute several programs to rekindle economic growth and save countless lives. The United States Government as well as state governments began to offer free rations to all who lived in El Paso as well as other war torn cities, including poor Mexican's. This created a swarm of Mexican's who owned no land to cross the Rio Grande River for this benefit. Many of them never returned to their homeland.

As Benjamin gradually began acquiring money, he was able to buy food to supplement what he raised. The only flour available in stores in El Paso Del Norte where they lived was full of weevils and worms and had a bitter taste. By the end of the war years, Benjamin was discouraged. His brother, Nehemiah "Nim" who was taking care of some of his properties, had chosen the Union side and when he saw all the property being taken by the Southern soldiers, he attempted to leave Texas and was shot and killed by Confederates. Benjamin began to feel that if he moved back to El Paso, he would have to start all over again. As an exiled American in Mexico, he knew he could have lost all of his holdings. His chance meeting of Mills, who was in charge of returning rightful property back to their owners, only resulted in angry stares as Mills was always for the Union and Benjamin was for the South. Benjamin had heard that Mills had gained considerable post war influence because of his stand for the Union. He began to realize that his anger and stubbornness toward Mills would get him nowhere. Mills was a Free Mason in good standing as was Benjamin. This gave them some common ground to work with.

The loss of his holdings in El Paso as well as the loss of his American Citizenship left Benjamin in utter discouragement. He had fought in the Mexican American War for his country and suffered greatly as a prisoner in a Mexico City prison. His allegiance was to his country and now, he had lost that unwillingly. Benjamin's thoughts were for his wife Juana and his two children. He couldn't bear to watch them live in near poverty.

He had to do something to show his allegiance to America and regain his rightful place in his beloved El Paso. This would take a humble attitude and a witty mind to regain the stature he once had. The result of all of Benjamin's plans to redeem himself resulted in a letter written to Mr. W. W. Mills, his one time friend who became an enemy during the war. He had no idea how Mills would react to it, but he had to take the chance anyway.

Paso del Norte, Mexico, Oct. 12th 1864

Mr. W. W. Mills:
Dear Sir -
You may think strange to receive a communication from me, but as circumstances alter cases I will proceed with my subject. I left Sherman, Texas on the 27th of December last with the intention of making my way, if possible, to El Paso, as I did not think my life safe in Texas out of the Confederate ranks, which service did not suit me. I came here with the full intention of crossing over to El Paso to live, if I could get admission by complying with all that might be required of a citizen. But when I arrived here I commenced to talk with some old friends, and changed my notion for a time. I am now tired of living a dog's life, and I wish to live on your side of the river. I hope you will pass over in forgetfulness any hard feelings you might have entertained toward me, and report favorably to the commanding officer at your post. Please let me hear from you by the bearer, and let this communication be confidential, and oblige, yours, etc.
B. S. Dowell

The bearer of the letter was ten year old Mary Dowell. Benjamin wanted his old pre-war friend to remember that he had a family to be concerned about and how precious a little girl she was indeed. The attempt to renew his friendship worked.

Mr. Mills immediately replied that he would be Benjamin's friend and invited him to his house. Since Mills had become a powerful force in El Paso, he didn't feel the need to check with Colonel George W. Bowie who was the commanding office of the post. This was a breach of etiquette Mills was now powerful enough to carry off.

The renewal of Benjamin and Mills friendship turned into a business deal concerning Benjamin's racing horse, Kit. They spoke of the possibility of racing Kit and making enough money to get back on their feet. As they planned their "rags to riches" scheme, a Union officer appeared at the door. The Union guard said he had orders to take Benjamin's mare Kit, he had brought with him. He was also ordered to arrest Benjamin and place him in the guard house. Mills was highly upset and replied "what, Federal bayonets shoved into my door after all I have gone through?" As far as Mills was concerned, it was an unwarranted attack on him. He went along with Benjamin and angrily confronted Colonel Bowie. He told him that Benjamin Dowell was ready to take the oath required in President Lincoln's amnesty proclamation, to regain his lost citizenship and place in America. Colonel Bowie was adamant about refusing Benjamin's citizenship. Bowie refused to permit his adjutant to administer the oath, but said as a favor to Mills, he would let Benjamin and his mare go back to Mexico.

When Benjamin crossed the border and went back to Mexico, Mills had worked out another plan to help his newly acquired friend. He wrote out the oath for renewal of his citizenship and had Benjamin swear to it before Henry J. Cuniffe, United States Counsel to Mexico and Paso del Norte. Then he triumphantly took Benjamin as a full fledged American Citizen before Colonel Bowie who took things in stride and accepted Benjamin as a citizen.

The accepted friendship by Mills, and the renewed citizenship allowed Benjamin to regain his valuable properties. Their worth was nominal at the time but increased considerably later on. Benjamin found his property in a trashed condition as his house, bar and store were used as officers quarters during the war. He felt it was a small price to pay, as many of his friends lost everything they owned.

In an apology to his fellow El Pasoan's, Mr. W. W. Mills reported that his act to give the United States Court of New Mexico jurisdiction over El Paso County was to help stop smuggling. This was due to the lack of United States Courts in Texas. He was given this power to act as the Collector of Customs. He had not realized that ultimately this Court procedure would involve the confiscation of real estate of his fellow El Pasoans. When the confiscation actions started, Mills protected the property of Benjamin Dowell and others, including the James Magoffin's family although his property was not returned until 1873, five years after his death.

Benjamin refused to accept defeat after finding his property thrashed. He had sold all of his bar fixtures during war time exile, but he began to rebuild by buying furnishings of John Woods' Franklin House hotel and bar which went out of business.

This included mirrors, pictures, chairs, tables and accessories. The demise of Woods bar was because he could not compete with the Lone Star Hotel and bar which had installed wood floors in 1868. The wooden floors were much preferred over the old dirt floors of the prior bar's and saloons in the area.

Chapter XV

"KIT", A SURE WINNER

The renewed friendship with Mills was partly based on a possibility that the two would be partners in racing Benjamin's mare, "Kit". The prospect for racing "Kit" was decided after she had won several small races along the border, and proved her ability to beat any horse she raced. The recall of many interesting races that had been run along Overland Street before the war left Benjamin and Mills dreaming of making a fortune. Benjamin would put up the horse Kit and his knowledge of racing horses, and Mills would put up the money for the stakes. He assured Mills that Kit could outrun any quarter nag that would come to El Paso! Mills trusted Benjamin's knowledge of horses he had picked up in his early years in Kentucky. He felt comfortable putting up the large sums of money that was to be placed on bets that Kit would race for. This was an opportunity, Benjamin thought, to regain his prominence in El Paso that was lost during the war.

The race track that was to be made famous by many horse races followed Overland Street to its junction with El Paso Street which is the downtown area of today. As the word got around about Kit's unbeatable races, competition began to pour in from around the local states, as they saw that Kit was the one to beat to gain recognition and fame.

Competition came mostly from California, New Mexico, and Colorado. There were beautiful horses that appeared much larger than Kit, yet couldn't keep up with her. For such a fast horse, Kit was friendly and seemed to love being around people. Benjamin would put his daughter Mary, who was twelve at the time, on Kits back and walk her around.

The news had reached most of the southern states and the West that Kit of El Paso, Texas, owned by Benjamin Dowell, was the fastest race horse in America!

Benjamin got the word that his partner, Mills was getting married and his wife to be didn't like gambling. This ended the partnership with Mills and left Benjamin to go it alone in 1869. The mare's most famous race was against Fly, owned by a man from New Mexico named Maxwell. Benjamin had advertised in the New Mexico newspaper, that he would race Kit a quarter mile against any horse for $2,000.00. When Maxwell delivered his horse named Fly to El Paso, Benjamin could see that Kit had her work cut out. Fly was a huge horse, who towered over Kit. She was a thoroughbred from Missouri. Fly was a bay and a little lighter in color than Kit. Mr. Maxwell claimed Fly was from Arabian Stock. Kit on the other hand was average in size, a dark bay with a small head, small ears and remarkably small hoofs. She was so gentle that Benjamin's children rode her. Benjamin told his rider to hold Kit back until she passed a row of trees about halfway down the course. Then he was to prod her with a touch of the quirt (a braided whip).

The challenge took place on January 6, 1872. People came from as far away as Santa Fe, New Mexico, and Chihuahua, Mexico. If they lacked money, they would put up their horses and cows for bets. Men who knew Maxwell, however, had the money to back his mare. People were walking along the track with hands full of bills, betting two and three to one on Fly. One observer figured as much as $25,000 changed hands that day. The backers of Fly felt confident that their mare would run away with the race. The citizens of El Paso and the surrounding area saw Kit run in previous races and felt assured that she would win. The Mexican crowd would yell out to Benjamin "Senior Don Benito, yo voy con usted" which meant, "Ben we are going with you!" The crowds began to grow as the time neared for the big race.

People on horse drawn "carretas" (buckboards) appeared and many on horseback and on foot. As the cheering crowd watched, the horses were brought out on the track.

The excitement was more than anyone could bear, as most of the crowd waited months for this occasion and traveled from afar.

The beautiful mares came side by side and were a sight to see, then a shout from the official "GO" after a short countdown was heard. The horses were "off" at a fast pace, leaving a cloud of dust behind them. As everyone stared in amazement, Fly took an early lead. This left Kit fans upset and disappointed as they didn't know the plan of holding Kit back until it was time to unleash her powerful strength. As Kit's rider was instructed to do, he stayed a few lengths behind the front runner and waited for the appointed time to let go. As the row of trees approached, Kit's jockey took out his quirt and began to lightly tap Kit from behind. The results were astonishing to all that watched, as Kit put on the speed and began to catch up with Fly. The rush that Kit exhibited kept growing as she caught up with Fly and began to pass her. The crowd began to roar with excitement and astonishment. Then in a moment of excitement, Kit's jockey turned around in his saddle as he passed Fly, thumbed his nose up and yelled out "shoo Fly!"

As Kit crossed the finish line several lengths ahead of Fly, the crowd went wild.

Many who had won money on their bets ran up to Kit and kissed her. The judges ruled that Kit came out about fifteen feet ahead to win. Maxwell was in shock as he found it hard to believe that Fly had been beaten. The money that changed hands from the "haves" to the "have nots" was welcomed as many of Kits fans were poor Mexicans. There was talk about racing Fly against Kit again at a later date, but Maxwell backed out after thinking it over and getting a better view of how fast Kit was. The word got out that Kit was unbeatable. This brought many race horses from far off places just to prove they could beat her, and make some money.

The last race Kit won, was an encounter with a Dutchman and his undefeated race horse. The stakes were high and it appeared like another big race much like the one with Fly. The outcome was the same, kit won, and many of El Paso's poor put up what little money they had to double their savings. In another incredible fast race, Kit showed everyone who was the fastest. The gallant mare who was loved by everyone living on both sides of the border, remained undefeated in all of her races over the years. Since Kit was so popular, many people would stop by Benjamin's place just to see her and pet her. They kept feeding her and encouraging her to eat more and more as a reward for all her victories. Little did they know that they were killing her, as she ate and ate to please everyone. The attention that Kit received went on without much notice that Kit was overeating. This later resulted in her getting sick and she died just three years after her race with Fly. The death of Kit was reported by many newspapers in several states. One of the largest being the Santa Fe Daily New Mexican dated July 16, 1875. Thus ended one of the most famous documented race horses in history.

The loss of Kit was upsetting to Benjamin and his family, as Kit was more than just a race horse, she was a pet who was ridden and loved by the kids in the area. Although Benjamin was attached to Kit, as she was the best, he also had two other race horses at the time. The horses became well known in the area. Their names were Solomon and Big Horse. It was Solomon, however who began to take Kits place in winning races. He was a giant stallion, yet was so gentle that children played around his feet.

One day, the ferry cable broke across the river connecting El Paso with Juarez Mexico. Solomon was used to hold the cable in place, while workman set a new anchor post to reconnect the cable. In a friendly jester of concern for the community, Benjamin offered his horse Solomon to help, as he was so large and strong. He had no idea that the strain would result in his death. The town of El Paso went into mourning, as Solomon was considered a hero. The loss brought an end to the horse racing career for Benjamin. He was never to reach the heights of prominence in horse racing circles again.

Fig. 27 Ferry Crossing Between El Paso and Juarez, Mexico

Chapter XVI

Education and Social Life
In El Paso

In early El Paso, there were no schools. Benjamin knew the value of a good education, and made sure his children were educated. Mary's first lessons were at home, given by Benjamin when he had time. When he could afford it, he hired tutors to teach Mary and later Juan, his second child. When the family moved to Paso del Norte during the Civil War, Mary was taught to read in English and Spanish by a tutor who would come to their house on a daily basis. A Frenchman by the name of Peter Lafayette started a small school that Mary attended for a short while. The young Negro girl who lived with the Dowell's, took Mary to school on a buckboard pulled by an old nag. The first school on the American side of the river that Mary attended, was taught by a Mr. Wright who's family lived on land Benjamin later owned in San Antonio, Texas in 1866. About this time, Nehemiah was born on April 24, 1866 in El Paso, Texas.

In 1867, an attorney by the name of M. A. Jones took up the teaching duties in a large building at Mesa and Main streets in El Paso. Mary described him as "a very nice gentleman and a Southerner".

When Mr. Jones became a judge, he continued to teach. Although he was said to have a weakness for spirits, he would not teach when he was drinking. Lacking a blackboard, he wrote the ABC's with his pencil on a white plaster wall of the classroom.

The first college trained teacher, Ms. Gaylord Clark who's husband was a judge, moved to town and became their teacher in 1868. She immediately attracted about twenty pupils, including several Mexican children. The classes taught were; reading, writing and arithmetic, a little history and fundamentals of Latin. The tragic shooting death of her husband in 1870 brought an end to her services as school mistress.

Her work was credited by Mary with laying the foundation for later school development in El Paso. Judge Clark and his wife had made it possible for Joseph W. Tays to come to El Paso as the towns first resident minister. In addition to his work with the Episcopal Church, he took over Mrs. Clark's little school. The minister opened his mission school November 1, 1870 with American and Mexican children attending. In 1871, Texas came under a compulsory school law and Parson Tays approached Mary Dowell, now nearly seventeen. "Mary", he explained, "the children are required to go to school now, and many of the Mexican families object to having their education taught to their girls by a man". Some of the girls were her own age.

Mary's efforts as one of El Paso's earliest teachers and her father's pioneer service to the community were recognized by the El Paso Board of Education when a school was named after him. The Ben S. Dowell School in northeast El Paso was named in honor of Benjamin Shacklett Dowell, and is located at 5249 Bastille Avenue in El Paso where it stands today.

Although education was important, there was also a social life that was much a part of early El Paso. The large aristocratic celebrations of the time, were generally for military hero's and honored dignitaries.

These celebrations were elaborate and festive, as they brought out all the sophisticated people who were the leaders of that time.

In November 1865, the American Army Officers wanted to honor Benito Juarez who later became President of Mexico. He had chosen Paso Del Norte, the town which was later to bear his name, as his military headquarters from August 15, 1865 until June 17, 1866, six months after the end of the Civil War. He drove the French with their Commander Maximillian out of Mexico. As his country fought the French in 1865, many stories of his bravery moved the military at Fort Bliss, Texas to honor him with a celebration. Juarez declined however, stating that "he resolved never to leave the soil of Mexico during its occupation by foreign invaders". The problem was easily solved, when a decision was made to move the celebration to Paso Del Norte, Mexico.

There were many balls, receptions, and entertainment over the years by residents from both sides of the river, including many military celebrations at Fort Bliss. For the celebration of Washington's birthday, February 22, 1866 the military again entertained and also gave recognition to the rebuilding of their fort which had been destroyed by Texas Confederates in 1861. Portraits of Washington, Lincoln and Benito Juarez occupied places of honor; Chinese lanterns illuminated the covered walkway to the dining hall. In a jester of friendship, Benito Juarez of Mexico was invited again, but declined since this would mean crossing the border. He sent his son and officials of his cabinet to attend in his place, as honored guests. There was also a written invitation to Benjamin and family as they were invited as well. Unfortunately Juana, Benjamin's wife was not feeling well and declined to attend. Benjamin decided that Mary who was eleven years old at the time, should go, as she was much a lady, who had been taught all the social graces. Benjamin told her "you must go, so in later years you can say you were at the dance were the Mexican Cabinet attended".

As Mary arrived with a family friend, a Mrs. Armijo who owned a dry goods store in El Paso, she noticed the Mexican and American flags that decorated the roof. The event had drawn people from as far as Las Cruces, New Mexico. In describing the event, Mary later recalled that Benito Juarez's only son was there.

She exclaimed "he was short and fat and looked like an Indian. He was nothing like I expected. I thought he would look like a prince in a fairy tale". In Mary's later memoirs, she commented further that she observed all the Mexican men with their waxed mustaches and all the fine silks and jewelry displayed by the ladies of El Paso del Norte. Everybody who was anybody was there including all the best families of El Paso and El Paso Del Norte, Mexico.

In later years Mary was to look back on the social events of the early days as a time when "ladies were ladies and gentlemen were gentlemen without any danger of mistaking a girl of good family, for a chorus girl or of a rough man's going, in good company". At social functions, no one exhibited rough manners. A gentleman bowed to his dancing partner and begged the honor of escorting her from her chaperone to the dance floor. Upon return, he bowed and gave his thanks to her.

> "The Grand Ball was typical of the elegant affairs. Dresses were of silk, made to stand by themselves. The women had dignity and their hair was crushed smooth on. The Grand Ball received much attention as ice was carried overland from New Mexico for such occasion. Orchestra's played until dawn, one starting up when another grew tired."

Benjamin and Juana attended many of the prominent social gatherings. Benjamin took Mary whenever possible and told her that the grand ball would be an occasion she would never forget. Throughout her long life, she agreed there was never anything like it in El Paso again.

Fig. 28   This Picture taken in 1868 is of Old Ft. Bliss near Franklin (now El Paso). It must have looked like this when Mary Dowell Phillips attended the evening of splendor.

Chapter XVII

Ben Dowell's El Paso

Benjamin's message to prepare for the future changes, due to prosperous growth from the coming railroad, began to payoff for him. He was seen as a man of vision and concern for his community. The ideas for change kept Benjamin busy, as he became the pied piper of El Paso. He wanted everyone to prosper, the well to do and the poor. This became his goal as he wanted "peace and good order as well as financial security for El Paso's citizens".

Once the city became incorporated, the need for a leader became apparent. The politicians of the day, attorneys, judges, landowners as well as merchants made up the five commissioners, Benjamin being among them. They were authorized to hold an election the second Tuesday in August, 1873. In that August 12th election, the 105 qualified voters chose Benjamin Dowell as Mayor. Six alderman were chosen also to work as his city cabinet. Three days later, Benjamin and his council met and organized.

Judge Joseph Magoffin then Precinct 1 justice of the peace, administered the oath of office. The council normally met at Benjamin's place of business, his saloon, but no drinking was allowed during business hours. Once the office of Mayor and Council were in place, the first order of business was a resolution adopted by the group to provide that the Mayor would also perform the duties of City Clerk.

The Mayor and Council chose the design of the city seal which became a five pointed star with the letters T-E-X-A-S between the points and the whole star surrounded by the words "City of El Paso, El Paso County". (The seal was later modified with a star in the center and "the City of El Paso" around it) If peace and good order were to be established, city ordinances had to be set. Ben knew that without law and order, his beloved El Paso would be doomed to failure. He saw how the lawless growing pains affected the well being of the city over the years.

In Benjamin's attempt to clean up the town, a fine was set at $100.00 for the crime of carrying concealed weapons. The same fine was also set pertaining to the crime of discharging firearms within the city limit "after sundown and before sunrise" with certain exceptions such as self defense or defense of property. Other crimes included; engaging in or encouraging or assisting in riots, public noise, disturbance or disorderly assemblies or assaults. The stealing and receiving and concealing stolen property. It was also forbidden to become intoxicated, to pitch pennies or to play marbles for keeps. These crimes were considered misdemeanors punishable by fine or imprisonment in the city prison. The first City Ordinance concerned management of the "acequias" (waterways). It became a misdemeanor for any person to bathe in the ditches. Persons were also forbidden to water their dogs, hogs, goats, horses, or cattle in the local ditches. Violators were to be tried before the Mayor's Court and could be fined up to $100.00.

Since the waterways were so important to the city, it became a misdemeanor to throw cigars or cigarette butts or trash into the "acequia" (ditches and canals). This also included livestock, which were forbidden to drink from the ditches or dam them up. The morals of the town were also looked after; it became illegal to swear in a saloon, to steal a neighbors property, to give a public dance without paying a $1.00 license fee.

The precious waterways became a big issue as Benjamin and his council attempted to improve the cities water supply. The care of the irrigation ditches was passed on to the citizenry living in the southwest of town, under what was known as the Alcalde System. The council decreed that every man eighteen and older must devote at least a day a year to clean and maintain the ditches and those who used the water from the ditches should work on them in proportion to the amount of water they used. When it came time for the annual ditch cleaning, nobody turned out. Being ordered by a city council did not set to well with them.

The water commissioners had the power to imprison those who failed to do their work, but it was impossible to jail all the men in town. It soon became apparent that taxes would have to be levied on the property owners and then hire workers to clean the waterways with the tax money. A November election amendment provided that the City would assess and collect one-fourth of one per cent of the amount assessed against all real estate in the city limits for the purpose of repairing waterways and bridges. In a short time of being Mayor, Benjamin began to accomplish much to improve living conditions and a safe and sane El Paso.

In the years that followed, Benjamin became a celebrity of sorts. Not only did he run the most popular watering hole in town, (Ben Dowell's Saloon) he was an owner, public official, grocer, rancher, and businessman. His demeanor and personality of an unexcitable, easy going, live and let live style allowed him to deal with every problem that came his way during thirty years of leadership and active citizenship in El Paso. It earned him the name of "Uncle Ben" affectionately dubbed by his fellow citizens. Benjamin's own saloon served a variety of civic functions over the years. A post office when he was postmaster, a polling place at election time and haven for countless traders and military officers who stopped in for billiards and all night card games. In his capacity as Mayor, he was instrumental in protecting and regaining some land, that Mexico tried to illegally claim for themselves.

The Rio Grande had been designated as the international boundary between the United States and Mexico, first by the Congress of the Texas Republic in 1836 and again in the 1848 Treaty of Guadalupe Hidalgo. The river changed its course between El Paso del Norte, Mexico, and El Paso, Texas several times between 1853 and 1863, then moved farther south after a severe flood in 1864. Mexico then claimed some three hundred acres of land that was North of the river on the American side. Since the treaty's never took in account the possibility that the Rio Grande would change its course, it remained that any change through flooding would naturally continue to remain the boundary. The Mexican Government tried desperately to regain the acreage they lost from the Rio Grande changing courses. When one of their plans failed to return the land to them, they set out on another devious plan; "to meet some parties in consultation, with a view of entering into some arrangement tending to the changing of the natural channel of the Rio Grande River against which I do most earnestly protest" wrote Benjamin to the Perfecto of El Paso del Norte, Jose Maria Uranga. "In his capacity as the Mayor of El Paso and a property owning citizen said Benjamin," "he felt it would be unlawful for the two city officials to effect a change in the international boundary". "That was, he stressed, the prerogative of the sovereign governments of the Republic of Mexico and the United States of America, and then only by treaty stipulations entered into in the proper form and manner".

Over three hundred acres were involved in this land transaction at the time. In Ben's patriotic view of what Mexico was trying to do, was to propose an artificial changing of the channel by placing dams or canals in violation of the treaty between the two governments. Benjamin and his council helped protect Americas interests by disallowing unethical practices by the Mexican Government to gain American soil illegally. It took nearly a century to completely solve this problem, through actions taken by Presidents John F. Kennedy and Adolfo Lopez Matoes in 1962. What was known as the Chamizal Convention, named for the area in question, straightened the river channel. As a result, 5,500 El Paso citizens were relocated to other parts of the city.

Although the final decision returned 630 acres to Mexico from the United States, 193 acres were returned from Mexico to the United States. I am sure if Benjamin had been around, it would have not been so favorable for Mexico, as he was a fighter for what he thought was right!

Benjamin's public career did not end with his one term as Mayor. He was elected a County Commissioner in 1878 and a City Alderman in 1880, all the while continuing to run his saloon, operate a ranch north of town, and hold high office in the Masonic fraternity.

CHAPTER XVIII

TIMES WERE GOOD

As Ben's family grew with the birth of Elijah (Lige) born April 1869 in El Paso, so did his holdings and financial empire. He was reaping the years of hard work and dedication to the townsfolk of El Paso, Texas. In 1872 as Ben spent his retired years on his farm near El Paso, his daughter, Mary, was becoming a socialite of sorts. She became involved in the social functions befitting a father who was Mayor of El Paso at one time. Her going and coming in and out of El Paso, as well as being a teacher and of a prominent family, left her pursued by many suitors.

It was Warner Phillips who caught Mary's eye however, as he was a learned man from a prominent family from Missouri. Although he was twenty years her senior and had been married before, Mary became very fond of him. Upon introducing him to Ben as a person of interest, the two became good friends. Ben grew to like Warner and approved of his courtship and subsequent marriage to Mary. Warner Phillips success as a son-in-law and his prominence in the community indicated that Mary made a wise choice. Since Mary was the "apple of Ben's eye", he didn't spare any expense in giving them a festive wedding ceremony. They gathered family members and all their prominent friends for a happy celebration.

Warner Phillips and Benjamin Dowell became close friends, Ben trusted Warner with guardianship of his will if anything should happen to him. He trusted Warner to be responsible for his boy's inheritance. In a gesture of love Ben had for Mary and her newly acquired marriage to Warner Phillips, he gave them some land in his upper valley holdings. They started a five acre ranch on that land, which was eight miles from town. They had the only dairy farm for fifty miles around.

By 1879 they had 100 head of cattle and sold their butter for fifty cents a pound in El Paso. In Warner Phillips own words, "he found the climate fine for stock and the country the best he had ever seen for chickens." As the farm grew and Mary's marriage prospered, Ben spent a lot of time in his retired years assisting his extended family in their ranch. In order to protect their cows, hogs, goats and chickens from varmints like mountain lions and coyotes, Ben ordered steel traps and placed them around the farm. He would bait them with chicken or fresh meat. The traps worked, and saved many cows from being killed by mountain lions. The traps also trapped beavers, a feat which Benjamin considered quite an achievement. In order to keep the coyote population down, you could pay taxes with the coyote scalps, which brought two dollars a piece off your property taxes.

Prior to Ben setting the animal traps, the ranch totally depended on their large dogs to keep away the wild animals. The dogs could control the coyotes, but a mountain lion was much too large and powerful for them! The menace of wild animal attacks on their livestock was not all they had to worry about. There were many Indians who were constantly seeking to destroy the white man's way of life. These tribes were not friendly and supportive of the pioneers as they settled in the outlying areas of El Paso. They were unlike the Tigua tribe who worked with the new settlers, to tame and improve the living conditions of the frontier. To deal with the on-going thefts and loss of his cattle, Ben branded all his cattle with a capital "J" and a capital "G" running together "JG". This worked well for him, as many settlers passing through the area were more concerned about being caught, if found with Ben's cattle. This could result in dire consequences. As the Ben Dowell ranch grew in livestock and in crops, so did Mary and Warner's ranch and farm as well. This wasn't all that was growing for them, as their family grew also.

Warner and Mary Phillips had two tow-headed boys who were near the ages of her younger brothers. Ben Dowell Phillips, who was named after her father, was born June 15, 1874 and John Newton Phillips was born March 13, 1877. As families were in those days; there were many siblings to help around the farm, it was not uncommon to see large families of a dozen children or more. A few years later, Warner and Mary had two more sons; Robert Bailey who was born February 7, 1880 the same year Ben passed away, and another son Ben never saw, Austin born January 28, 1886. Unlike many families in those days, hardships and disasters were not uncommon. Warner and Mary were blessed with a fifth child, they named, Juanita, after Ben's wife Juana. She was the image of her mother, Mary. On one very sad day, she drowned in a nearby canal which were called acequia's, as a small child. The pain of losing her only daughter, I am sure, was the worst pain of all, Mary and Warner had to endure. This brought an end to the growth of their family. I am sure the incident was too long in getting over and affected their decision to refrain from having any more children.

When Mary's two older son's, Ben and John, were young boys ages six and three, Ben would sometimes wake up in the morning and tell his wife, "I dreamed of my little tow heads, I am going to see them". He would hitch up a wagon and drive to the ranch to see the grandchildren, who would run to meet him when they saw him approaching. He would put them in the wagon and bring them to the house.

Ben would always bring his youngest son, Richard (Dick), who was a year younger than Mary's Ben along with him on visits. On many occasions, Elijah and Richard, Ben's youngest sons would spend a great deal of time at Mary's ranch. They enjoyed playing with Mary's boys. As time permitted, Mary held school for her brothers and taught them how to pray. They attended the Catholic church in Juarez, Mexico and sometimes the priest visited their home for a rosary service. Ben's youngest son, Dick, liked to ride horses, more so than the older brothers. Once he fell off his horse and was dirty and dazed. His father asked him "you had enough?" to which Dick replied "no! Put me on the horse again." Ben was well pleased. He wanted his boys to be manly and despised anything effeminate about any man.

There were many hunting and camping trips, where Ben took the boys and showed them how he learned to survive and enjoy the wilds of the forest. His later years on the ranch were all about spending time with his family. He would expect his son's to help around the ranch, as he himself was expected to as a young boy. When time permitted however, he was always spending time roughing it out in the wilds with his boys, so they would know how to survive and make the best of what they had. In retrospect, it was a tough break to family and friends, to lose such a wonderful person as Ben at such an early age. I believe things would have been better in the lives he touched with his love, humor, and strong character if he had lived longer.

The final years of Ben's life were full of days with his beloved wife, Juana, family, and friends. The grandchildren Mary brought into his life, insured his legacy would go on into the future. His four boys would also carve out their own destiny with children of their own. Ben was indeed a happy, successful man. He looked around and saw all the good he had done for his town of El Paso. He knew the railroad would reach them in a few years, bringing thousands of pioneers seeking a new life out West.

He spoke of and lived as though he could see El Paso becoming one of the great cities of the West. This left him pleased of what he had accomplished in the early days of El Paso's history. The same loving care and attention he gave to the citizen's of his beloved El Paso, was also given to his wife and children. The retired years Ben experienced were full of camping out with his boys and local picnics with Juana. The entire family, as well as his extended family of Mary and her husband, Warner, and boys, gave Ben a sense of pride and joy as they all loved the outdoors. The desire to explore and the pioneering spirit Ben portrayed and lived, was passed on to his loved ones. He spent the last days of his life re-living his past in stories and time spent raising live stock, crops and enjoying the outdoors.

Ben left a legacy of faith in God and love of Country, as he treated people with respect and concern for their welfare. His patriotism knew no bounds, as he fought for his Country in the Mexican-American War as well as the Civil War. The time and effort he gave to creating a town of peace, tranquility and welfare for its citizens, gave El Paso its start in becoming one of the great cities of America. The end to such an outstanding life and career came all too soon. His life was cut short at the age of sixty-two. The ironic circumstances surrounding his death are surprising. The imprisonment in a Mexican prison and subsequent torture, as well as a long involvement in the Civil War were survived by Ben. The threats of wild Indians on his journey's as well as his life in early El Paso, full of gun slingers was always a daily threat. In spite of all he had lived through, he survived to retire and enjoy life with his family.

Then, on one cold day November 5, 1880, just three weeks prior to his sixty second birthday, he was out in his fields in the river valley above

El Paso. As he rode through the fields he heard water running and discovered a leak in an irrigation ditch. He knew that if the leak was not repaired it would eventually flood a vineyard, possibly ruining the crop. There were many times he would overwork himself to complete a job, with no concern for his own health. On this day, it was no exception. In a moment of decision, Ben jumped off his horse and into the cold water. He spent a long time sweating in exhaustion, in knee deep water, shoveling dirt to stop the leak. He was so pre-occupied with the work at hand, he failed to be concerned with his own health. He got a bad chill from the cold November air and dampness. The ride back to his home through the cold weather, and being wet, was more than his old body could take.

His loving, caring Juana put him to bed and tended to him. He reluctantly stayed in bed and tried his best to recover from the weak condition he sank into. But, as the days passed, he worsened and caught pneumonia. After three days in bed, Ben began to realize that he may not survive. He called the children in to see him, one by one. The thought of leaving his beautiful family, due to his carelessness, left him saddened and tearful. The same prosperity that made him so prominent, his wealth in business and farms, brought about his own demise. Yet, he left them with word of God's love for them as well as his own. To his boys he asked for obedience to their mother. To be of good character and honesty, as well as love for God. He called for Mary, his only daughter whom he deeply loved and cherished. As he had laid in bed for three days, he told her it was clear that he had pneumonia. In a soft voice he said, "I'm going to die, Mary. I've never been in bed for three days in all my life!" As Ben slowly got worse, and spent hours saying good bye to family and friends, he died quietly in his home on November 8, 1880. He was buried in the Masonic Cemetery whose site he had obtained six years earlier.

At the December 1ˢᵗ meeting, the City Council passed a resolution which read:

> Resolved that in Mayor Dowell we recognize a man of character, fully alive and Deeply devoted to the material interest of this section, just and honorable in his dealings with others, generous as a neighbor and a friend, and a kind and affectionate husband and father.

The Masonic Lodge minutes carry a Memoriam of the death of the pioneer member:

> Brother B. S. Dowell died at his residence in El Paso, Texas on Monday, November 8, 1880 at 7 p.m. Buried with Masonic honors by El Paso Lodge Tuesday, November 9, 1880. Brother H.R. Brinkerhoff officiating. Brother B. S. Dowell was one of the founders of El Paso Lodge 130 holding honorably the position of District Deputy Grand Master at the time of his death. He was a true and respected Mason, and his loss is deeply felt.

Benjamin, from all indication was a man of God, with high morals and strong character. He taught his children the customs and social graces of the day, as well as the Christian faith. He also instilled in them a love of Country and the love for our Lord. Many of his best friends were men of the cloth. His dealings with others was always beyond reproach. He strived to make El Paso, his beloved town, an example of a good moral and safe harbor for everyone.

Chapter XIX

Ben's Fraternal Order

There were times when Ben was on the verge of financial destitution. His faith and strong spiritual beliefs, as well as helpful friends, saved him from ruin.

One of his influential friends, Mr. W. W. Mills, used his authority to help Ben regain his citizenship and property. This occurred after the Civil War had forced Ben to take his family across the border into Mexico for their protection. The only hope Ben had of returning to El Paso and regaining his property, was through the assistance of Mr. Mills who was appointed as the Collector of Customs by the Union Army after the war was over. It was Ben's past friendship, as well as their mutual membership in the ancient Free and Accepted Masons that brought them together and renewed Ben's return to El Paso, and his rightful place in the community.

The return of Ben's property and status, was also helped along by his willingness to share his race horse "Kit" in a business deal with Mr. Mills. They would race "Kit" with Ben using his training expertise and knowledge of horses and Mr. Mill's putting up the money for the bets on "Kit" to win. Since the Free Mason credo is; fellowship, integrity and good citizenship, they are pledged to help one another in time of need. It was no doubt that Ben's connection as a member of the Free Masons, was a primary factor in the decision made by Mr. Mills who was also a member. It is interesting to note that Ben's father, James Board Dowell, was a "Freemason". He apparently was involved in this fraternal order as it was passed along from father to son all the way from previous generations in England.

The Freemason Fraternal Organization was originally steeped in mysticism. The traditions were a mixture of historical fact and legend. Freemasonry had developed over many centuries and relied heavily on notions inherited from the customs and practices of the stonemason's of medieval times. Freemasonry is the oldest and largest fraternal organization in the world. It is a universal society of friends who seek to become better people through their association with one another. This organization can be traced to the beginning of the Master Mason's who created the great churches and cathedrals of medieval Europe; some say that its birth was linked to the Knights Templar, a military and religious Order of Warrior Knights who rose to prominence at the time of the crusades, others say it goes back to the time of King Solomon's temple which was built by them in Jerusalem, if not before.

Freemasonry is not a religion, though it holds to many Christian ideals of brotherly love, the Mason's must be tolerant, respectful, kind and understanding. They must practice charity, and commitment to philanthropy and truth. The essential qualifications all Mason's must share is a belief in a single Supreme Being. The Mason's are to be of good character and repute. Freemasons are a fraternal order; who received the name from stonemasons, builders of Europe's cathedrals. They were an elite class that could travel freely between countries, unlike serfs who's movements were carefully restricted, hence the term, "Freemason" came into being.

In the eighteenth century, during a period of history known as the "Enlightenment", the lodges began to accept members who were not stonemasons. Among their members were men like Wolfgang Amadeus Mozart, Johann Wolfgang, Von Goethe, Frederick the Great and George Washington.

Surely the ideals that were a part of Freemasonry were instilled in young Benjamin Shacklett Dowell. He was noted for fairness, compassion for others as well as a desire to do what was right to benefit others. The title given to him by his friends and towns folk was "Uncle Ben", this attests to the friendly, helpful ways he dealt with the public. His sympathetic ear and willingness to help those in need were his trademark.

CHAPTER XX

SLAVERY IN AMERICA

The displacement of humanity for another's sake is despicable. The plight of the African slave as they were brought to America, was inhumane and barbaric. The unsanitary conditions, disease, hunger, and depression claimed the lives of over fifty percent of those who began the journey. Once the slaves realized they would never return home to Africa, they attempted to make the best of their sad condition. Their options were few and their struggle had taken a new turn. They began to realize that for them to survive, they had to comply with their captors and make the best of living with the Americans.

As many immigrants landed in Virginia from the old country, they found slavery to be a common way of life, especially in the southern states. Although the Declaration of Independence of 1777 decreed that, "all men are created equal", this did not change slavery in the South. The Northern states where society was based on an industrial economy, had less of a need for slaves, and even found the idea repugnant. In the Southern states however, it was a different story, as their large plantation crops needed slaves to work the fields. The Northern states outlawed the practice of keeping human chattels by 1804. The Southern states however, defended the institution of slavery, claiming that slaves were private property and protected by law. Although there were many mistreated slaves, the larger majority were domestic help in the plantation homes and became well treated family servants. This is not to say I condone slavery, but to underscore the socially acceptable way of life at the time.

The choice to purchase a slave was not as easy as one would think. As a slave owner there came many responsibilities. If you were able to afford the luxury of having a slave, you accepted this person with the knowledge that for better or worse he or she was your responsibility. The emotional and physical health of your new family servant was important. If treated fairly and decently, the mutual agreement between the two owner and servant could in many ways benefit both. Although there were initial problems encountered with such an institution. The social practice became some what acceptable to both parties. This allowed for a more give and take relationship between the two. The partnership, although sometimes strained, in many cases the slaves became extended family members. They (the slaves) became privy to the owners financial, economical and personal problems. As strange as it may sound, upon gaining freedom to leave their owners, many chose to stay and be paid for their services.

Since slavery was well entrenched and accepted during the early pioneering days of Kentucky and other Southern states, it was no surprise to learn of my families heritage in dealing with this social issue. It was a known fact that James Board Dowell and Barbara Shacklett Dowell had purchased slaves for themselves and family members.

As indicated in family history, it was stated that they would give 2 slaves of theirs to the newly weds in their family, as a gift. This was usually for the marriages of their children.

However, James who was the son of James B. Dowell chose to sell or give his slaves to his brother Nehemiah. A reason was never given, but Nehemiah favored the Union and this may have been a statement regarding his feelings on slavery. In other records it was indicated that Susan Dowell Shacklett, wife of Bernice B. Shacklett, brought a young black girl who was a slave, with them when they moved to El Paso, Texas from Kentucky. She was later sold to her brother, Benjamin S. Dowell. In Mary Dowell Phillips memoirs, it was indicated that the young black girl took her to school in a buckboard each day when they lived in Juarez, Mexico during the Civil War. She also stated, "that after the negro girl grew up, she left".

Chapter XXI

Benjamin and Juana's Children and Legacy

Benjamin and Juana had five children they dearly loved. Their first child, Mary, was born Mary Marquez Dowell on October 30. 1854 in Los Angeles, California. She past away in El Paso Texas in 1951. Mary was the apple of Benjamin's eye. He gave her all the education she needed to prepare herself for the prominence she later received.

He began her education at an early age, when Mary was only six and taught her himself for over a year. Then, he made sure she had teachers and tutors, who would come to the house when no schools were available. Mary was considered a very intelligent pupil and displayed an ability to learn and use her knowledge to help others, as she taught young kids, who in some cases were older than she was. She married Warner Phillips around 1874. They had five children.

Benjamin and Juana's second child was John R. Dowell, known as Juan. He was born in August, 1862 in Ysleta, Texas. He past away in 1916. Little is known of John, other than he married a Lucia G. His death was recorded in the Sacred Heart Catholic Church in El Paso, Texas, and he was buried in Concordia.

Their third child was Nehemiah Dowell (Nim), born on April 24, 1866 in El Paso, Texas. It is not known when he passed away. It is believed that he married a Tigua Indian and that his sister, Mary was not fond of her. He had one child named Marie who was born in Anthony, Texas. After Nehemiah's wife passed away, Marie was very young and Nehemiah's sister, Mary, took her and raised her. Marie later listed her mother as Isabel, on her social security application. It was not known why her father, Nehemiah, did not raise her. When Marie grew up, she married a soldier from Fort Bliss by the name of Frank Hermanson. There is currently a great granddaughter named Peggy Hermanson Glover still living. In a story written in the El Paso Times dated February 14, 1893 and April 15, 1893 an obituary for a Gilan (John) Jean, an old Frenchman of Hueco Tanks, was found floating in the Rio Grande terribly mutilated. A Dick Wilson was eventually arrested, previously arrested was Mr. Charles Rhoduis and Nim Dowell.

We have no knowledge of the outcome.

Benjamin and Juana's fourth child was Elijah Dowell born April, 1869 in El Paso, Texas. He past away in Carlsbad, New Mexico, Eddy County on December 15, 1937.

His wife was Viola C. Hewitt (no other information known about her). They had one child, Edward Dowell, born July 7, 1895 in Houston, Texas. Edward passed away on June 11, 1979 in Riverside, California.

The last child born to Benjamin and Juana was Richard Dowell, born about 1875 in El Paso, Texas. His date of death is unknown. He married a lady named Refugio and moved to Mexico. No other information is available about him.

Although there was little information on John (Juan), Nehemiah and Richard, the two children who's lives were well documented were

Mary and Elijah. After Mary married Warner Phillips in 1870, they had four boys and a daughter. They were all born on their farm near El Paso, Texas. Their first child was Benjamin Dowell Phillips born June 15, 1874. The next child was John Newton Phillips born on March 13, 1877, and died February 7, 1953. Their third child was Robert Bailey Phillips. Their fourth son was Austin Phillips born January 28, 1886. Their last child was Juanita, no doubt named after her grandmother, Juana. She drowned in Ysleta in a small irrigation ditch called acequias, as a small child.

Mary and Warner's two older sons remained in El Paso throughout their lives.

Benjamin Dowell Phillips married Dolores Campos on September 4, 1907. They had two sons; Dr. Benjamin Austin Phillips who is on the staff of the University of Texas Medical Branch in Galveston. Ben Dowell Phillips died at 83 on January 13, 1958, just a few months after he and his wife celebrated their fiftieth wedding anniversary.

He had retired four years earlier after thirty-four years with the County Auditors Office in El Paso, Texas. John Newton Phillips, second son of Mary and Warner married Aurelia Gameros on September 24, 1898. They had four children, one daughter, Aurelia M. (Chella),born August 29, 1901 and Robert Warner, born August 1, 1911, as well as two more sons, John and Robert Austin. Aurelia (Chella) passed away June 14, 1995, after living all her life in El Paso. "Chella" Phillips served as Manager of El Paso Tennis Club from 1954 until her retirement in 1966 and held the El Paso City tennis championship for eight years. Robert Warner Phillips, an expert gunsmith, served as a Captain in World War II under General George S. Patton in the 2nd armored Division in Europe. He is currently 96 years old and living in El Paso. He has two daughters, Patty Snyder who lives in Houston, Texas (Pearland) and Mary Jane Leonard who lives in El Paso.

The other sons of Mary and Warner Phillips did not remain in El Paso; Robert Bailey Phillips was a Civil Engineering graduate of the University of Michigan at Ann Arbor. He married Lyle Roberts of Arizona and they had two children, Robert Bailey Jr. who died at about age fifteen and Lyle Arizona, now Mrs. Leroy Frankard of Pacific Grove, California. Robert Bailey Phillips died February 2, 1973. Austin Phillips, the couples fourth son, lost touch with his family. He was last known to be living in Peoria, Illinois in 1951.

After Warner Phillips death on November 15, 1887, Mary married Gaudencio Prieto in 1892. They had two children, G.D. Prieto of San Francisco, California and Mrs. Harold (Rose) Poppenhusen of Houston, Texas. This marriage did not last, however, and they divorced. Mary resumed the surname of Phillips.

Benjamin and Juana's first child Mary, and their third child Elijah, can be traced through most of their lives. Their life stores are filled with family members that have pioneered their own way to success, in their own right. The Mary Dowell Phillips family tree, is exemplified in Benjamin's great, great, great granddaughter, Tammie Michelle Snyder's school report dated December 8, 1997. (refer to appendix).

The history of Elijah Dowell was more difficult to research, as he traveled much and left few signs of his whereabouts. As far as the Dowell's and extended families were concerned, Elijah had drifted off into the sunset and was never heard from again. The rumors of his imprisonment and cowboy life, as he spent most of his time under the sky, was all they knew. The truth that was recorded in historical documents revealed so much more. The knowledge of Elijah's son, whom he named Edward, has added hundreds of Aunts, Uncles, Nieces and Nephews as well as first, second and third cousins to the already large Dowell Clan in America. From the Edward Dowell family's simple beginnings in Lakewood, New Mexico to Carlsbad, New Mexico, to

Arizona and eventually to California, they traveled and thrived. The difficult hardships, gave them the ambition to succeed in life. Their success came through hard work, education and our unshakable love of God.

Some of the Edward Dowell family became soldiers who fought for their country. They helped build the nation, as construction workers, railroad workers, aerospace and prison workers (Peace Officers). The love of family, God and country is evident in their lives and their children. The family has carried the torch that was handed down from our Grandpa Elijah and his ancestor's the Dowell's, and from our father, Edward.

The discovery of our ancestry and current relatives, has been a life long quest, as the knowledge of who they were and where they lived, eluded my family until now. The recent discovery of family through the internet and trips to El Paso, Texas and Meade County, Kentucky has been amazing and rewarding. We have had the pleasure to meet friendly and helpful relatives, as we sought to discover our ancestry. From the Benjamin Dowell Grammar School in El Paso, Texas to the Dowell farms in Meade County, Kentucky, the testament of their accomplishments abound. The "Bro-Kin Branch" has been mended, and the rightful place of the Edward Dowell Family has been restored and for my family of today, and tomorrow, this book is your ancestral story.

Chapter XXII

Elijah, Benjamin Shacklett Dowell's Fourth Child And His Legacy

Benjamin and Juana's fourth child, Elijah, was born in El Paso, Texas in 1869. He was preceded by Nehemiah and followed by Richard, their last child. Although initial records were scant about his life, research has revealed much, that had been previously unknown. The upheaval of the family after the death of his father, Benjamin was devastating and changed Elijah's life for the worse. He couldn't pick up the shattered pieces left by the family's loss. It left him angry and bewildered, like many young children who lose a loving parent.

The boys were forced to move to Ysleta, Texas and the Indian reservation as Juana, their mother, chose to return to her parents to live. The decision she made proved to be disastrous for her family. It affected her children in ways they never recovered from. To be living in a prominent, comfortable home with loving parents, then seemingly out of nowhere losing it all, is devastating to young children. Unfortunately, Juana was unable to deal with the painful loss of her husband and needed the comfort of her parents and childhood surroundings. The results of this transition left her proud and opinionated boys to face a new way of life they were unaccustomed too.

It is only a supposition as to what the boys had to deal with, living on an Indian reservation. The loss of close friends, and the positive influence their sister, Mary, had in their lives was truly felt, I am sure. In those days, as even today, there are social clashes between full blooded Indians and other ethnic backgrounds. The stigma of being half Indian and half Anglo left many referred to as a half-breed. This left the boys unaccepted by some Indians and Anglo's alike. This drastic change affected Elijah to the degree that he sought to make his own way in life, without the guidance of a strong prominent family he once had. It left him to his own choices, as school, education and proper social ways became foreign to him. The call of a tough cattle driving cowboy, was his choice to live.

He felt comfortable in the saddle, as his beloved father, Benjamin, taught him to ride at an early age. Unfortunately, Elijah and his brothers were too young to fully grasp and understand the qualities of their prominent father. Their guidance and thirst for knowledge was cut short by their father's untimely death. As they grew into young men, it was the harsh and wild West that became their teacher.

Elijah was left searching for his place in the sun, only to find himself in prison for his efforts. According to records, he only had himself to blame, as he was found guilty of horse theft and sentenced to five years hard labor at the Huntsville Texas Penitentiary. This was not until after he had married a young lady by the name of Viola C. Hewitt. In documented records of his incarceration, it was noted that he was married with no children upon commencing his sentence on June 27th, 1895. This was correct, as his son, Edward, was not born until July 7, 1895, ten days after his incarceration. In the 1900 Census, Elijah was still in prison but listed as single. Being left without a father upon his birth, Edward Dowell was left with only his mother, Viola C. Hewitt

Dowell to care for him. Their were no records of my father's birth mother that could be found. We can only assume that either she past away at an early age or from lack of ability, gave my father, Edward, up for foster care.

In a World War I Draft Registration dated July 4, 1917 it listed my father, Edward at age 21 and living with his father, Elijah Dowell in Lakewood, Eddy County, New Mexico. It also noted that he was supporting his father who was ill. The document was proof that they had found each other before 1917. The reason for their living in Lakewood, New Mexico, could have been due to some land his sister, Mary Dowell Phillips, owned at one time. She either gave the few acres of land to Elijah or sold it to him. The Mary Dowell Phillips memoirs indicated she lived in Lakewood, New Mexico at one time and raised peaches there. It is also noted that her grandson, Robert Phillips, indicated that Mary had mentioned living in Lakewood at one time. Another census in 1920 revealed that my father, Edward, was married to Estella Dominguez Dowell, my Mother, and Elijah my grandfather was living with them.

It was in Lakewood, New Mexico where all my older brothers and sisters were born. They could recall our grandfather Elijah bringing them fruit and vegetables he found in throw away bins behind food markets. They loved the old man they called "Grandpa" and listened to his cowboy adventures he told of his youth. In 1937 my grandfather Elijah became ill. He was admitted to the nearest hospital, which was in Carlsbad, New Mexico. He remained there for several months until his death on December 15, 1937. He was truly missed by everyone.

Elijah's rocky and unstable life, left a child behind, that he was later to search for and find. Their uniting and subsequent bonding was truly amazing, as years had passed after Elijah was released from prison before they would find each-other. The historical documentation discovered, gave us reason to believe that at the time of their getting together, Elijah was ill and his son, Edward, nursed him back to health. Since Edward was his only son, the two, I am sure, felt that it was them against the world. Elijah's relationship with his own family was strained and eventually ties were broken. His only closeness to anyone was his son, Edward. Their love for one another brought them close and left a "grandpa" all the Dowell family in Lakewood were proud of and loved.

In 1938 our family moved near Carlsbad, New Mexico, where my younger brother, Richard and I were born. I was born in February, 1942 and my younger brother, Richard was born February, 1943. My father bought a small farm in Happy Valley, a small out of the way settlement, where he tried to grow a large garden for the family. I recall our stock as being two old mules, a pig, a cow, some goats and geese. I enjoyed the animals, until one day my mother was milking our cow. I was later told that one of our mules, scared the cow, causing the cow to spill the can of milk. My mother yelled for someone to chase the mule away. I was nearby and hearing her crying out, grabbed a stick and chased the mule. To my surprise, the mule kicked me in the forehead rather than leaving the scene. I required eighteen stitches to close up the massive gash. For a three year old, it was quite an ordeal.

The journey for my father, Edward Dowell from Houston, Texas to El Paso, Texas to Lakewood, New Mexico, to Carlsbad, New Mexico, was not over. Soon after the war in 1946, our family moved to Phoenix, Arizona. The reasons for leaving were many I am sure, but the underlying struggle for a well paying job eluded my father. He worked for the railroad, and in the pot ash mines of New Mexico. The work was hard and the allotment check the family received from my brother, Robert who had been a soldier in World War II, was no longer being received. My father and my mother, Estella Dominguez Dowell, gave birth to twelve children.

This is a chronological list of the children:

Their first child was Elijah. He was the first child named after our grandfather. He was born in February, 1920. He passed away at the young age of 3 years and 6 months old in 1923.

Their second child was Lucille, born December, 1923. She married Fred D. Nelson and had seven children, one of whom was Freddy Nelson, the subject of a book I wrote titled "Born without Wings" in 2007. Lucille passed away in 1999.

Their third child was Robert Bob Dowell born May, 1925. He married Lucy Dominguez and they had four boys.

Their fourth child was Newton, born 1926 and died March 3, 1927.

Their fifth child was Edward (Eddie) born in April, 1928. He married Evelyn Embry and they had 3 girls.

Child number six was Lola born May, 1930. She married Thomas Brawdy, and they had three children. She later divorced and married George Nielsen and they had one child.

The seventh child was Rosy Lee born July, 1932. She married Juan Sandoval and had five children.

The eighth child was Martha who was born in 1931 and died on September 8, 1936.

Child number nine was Ethel born October, 1934. She married Elvin T. Davis and they had two daughters.

Their tenth child was Dorothy Mae, born June, 1936. She married Bill Killian and they had four children.

I was number eleven and I was born in February, 1942. I married Carole Jackson and we had two children. We later divorced, and I am currently married to Jane Steele Dowell.

Their twelfth and last child was Richard D. born in February, 1943. He Married Linda Wheatcroft and they had two children.

Elijah Dowell
1869-1937

Chapter XXIII

Edward and Estella Dominguez Dowell's Legacy

This is the legacy from the marriage of Edward and Estella Dominguez Dowell:

Their first child, Elijah Dowell died in 1923.

Their second child, Lucille Dowell Davidson, had seven children born to her union with Fred D. Nelson, now deceased. The remaining members of her family are four children; John Henry, Diana, Janie and Gloria Nelson.

Child number three was Robert Dowell and he was a soldier who fought in the Philippine Islands during World War II. He married Lucy Dominguez which resulted in four boys, and several grandchildren. One child, Able Dowell, survives the family today.

Child number four, Newton, passed away in 1927.

Their fifth child is Eddie Dowell. He has been married to Evelyn Embry for sixty years. They have three daughters; Donna, Cheryl and Patsy. Eddie is a retired carpenter and cement contractor, who helped build the city of Riverside, California for many years.

Child number six was Rosy Dowell, who married Juan Sandoval. They had five children. Their oldest daughter, Delphina Lopez, is a retired Correctional Officer rising to the level of Associate Warden at the Delano State Prison, California. Her two oldest sons, John and David work in the aircraft industry, as did their mother. Rosy's youngest son, Joseph is a cement worker and part time preacher. Her youngest daughter, Stella, and her husband operate an R.V. repair and service business. Rosy also has many grandchildren. Rosy later married Frank Silva.

Their seventh child, Lola Dowell, Nielsen, had three children in her first marriage to Thomas Brawdy, now deceased. They were Daniel, Marilyn, and Ronald. Ronald has worked for the City of Riverside for over thirty years. Lola's marriage to George Nielsen included a stepdaughter, Debbie. They had one child in the marriage, Michael. George Nielsen was a retired aircraft worker and has since past away. Their family also includes many grandchildren.

Their eighth child was Martha and she died in 1936,

Child number nine was Ethel Dowell and she had two daughters, Sandra and Janet, to her first marriage to Elvin Davis, now deceased. Ethel was a social worker for many years. Several grandchildren are also noted. She later married Paul Lara.

Their tenth child was Dorothy Dowell, mother of four; Barbara, Billy Joe, Ricky and Steve Killian born to her marriage to Bill Killian, now deceased. Many grandchildren are in their family also. Dorothy was the first female Correctional Officer to work at an all male facility, California Institution for Men, Chino, California in 1973.

I was child eleven named after grandpa Elijah. I am now known as James Robert Dowell. I was born on February 9, 1942 in New Mexico. I am also the author of this book. After living a hard life on a farm near Bakersfield, California since 1946, I graduated from South High School in 1960. After high school, life became much improved, as I became a data analyst for T.R.W. Systems, Redondo Beach, California and enrolled in college. I had the good fortune to work on a program; Lunar Excursion Module and the worlds first controllable rocket engine, which was utilized to land our astronauts on the moon. A young marriage to Carole Jackson, resulted in two children, Eileen and Eric. Eileen's marriage to Peter, an engineer from Australia has produced three boys and a girl. Upon completion of the moon landing in 1969, I began a new career with the California Department of Corrections. My first assignment was death row, supervising the Manson Women, (followers of the notorious Charles Manson). I was the first male Correctional Officer to work in an all female prison, California Institution for Women in Fontera, California. I rose to the level of a Supervising Counselor II after working at several prisons. I retired in 1994 after 24 years of service. I am currently employed part time in a Care Center for emotionally troubled children. I divorced in 1969 and raised my two children alone for ten years, before marrying Jane Steele Marshall in 1979. Our family included four children, as she had two daughters, Lisa and Kristen from a previous marriage.

Edward's twelfth and last child was Richard Dowell, a retired conductor/brakeman for the Great Northern Railroad. He married Linda Wheatcroft and they had two children, Doug and Pamela. Richard's wife, Linda, is a teachers aid. Their son, Doug, is completing his Masters Degree in business. He plans to teach language in South Korea. Their daughter, Pamela was a music teacher for many years and has recently promoted to Vice Principal of a grammar school.

Fig. 29　Edward Dowell (Author's Father) in about 1930

Fig. 30   Estella & Edward Dowell (Author's Parents) in about 1950

Fig. 31   Edward and Estella Dowell's Legacy (Approx. 1980)

Two Empty Chairs Symbolizing Mom and Dad

Back Row: Terry Cromwell, David Sandoval, Rosy Sandoval, Terry Sandoval,
                  Stevie Killian, Stella Santoya, Gary & Donna Hanley, Dorothy Dowell,
                  Jean Dowell, Bob Dowell, Jane Dowell, James Dowell, Ronnie Brawdy

Row 2:   John Sandoval,Jr., Janet Davis, Barbara Hemminger, Sandy Cromwell,
                  Jimmy Embry, Cheryl Silva, Evelyn Dowell, Theresa Madson,
                  Eddie Dowell, Patsy Madson, Sonya, Delphina Lopez, Patty Brawdy,
                  Mike Nielsen

Row 1:   Linda Dowell, Joe Hemminger, Andrea Santoya, John Sandoval,
                  Nicole Lopez, Andy Lopez

Front row: Leslie Silva, Dog (Sissy), Frank Lopez, Brian Sandoval

Missing: Richard Dowell, Lola and George Nielsen, Lucille and Ed Davidson

CHAPTER XXIV

A LOST GRANDMOTHER
REVEALS HERSELF

The search for my grandmother was over, with a good idea of who she was, or so we thought. The pieces came together so well, we felt comfortable with the mother we had chosen for my father. Then, after two months of anxiously awaiting for a response from Social Security administration, a letter was received in the mail. The request for a Social Security application by my father, was the only chance of ever knowing for sure, what my grandmother's maiden name was. This was due to a lack of a birth certificate, as the hall of records in Austin, Texas indicated they could not find one.

My "gum shoe" wife however refused to give up her search, as she knew the usual protocol for filing for a Social Security application required the information pertaining to applicants father, and mothers maiden name. The suspense of knowing what we waited for so long to know, was more than she could bear. Although I was out on an errand at the time, she couldn't wait to open the letter. In the letter, my wife found a copy of my dad's application for a social security card. It had been written on May 1, 1939. In the section marked "mother's full maiden name, whether living or dead" was typed Viola C. Dowell in error, as they had marked it out. Then next to it was her maiden name, Viola C. Hewitt.

In a strange twist of fate, the error that was still readable even though it was marked out, indicating; Viola C. Dowell, proved to us that my dad's father and mother were married. This was important, as we could find no record of their marriage certificate. My little "gum shoe" couldn't wait to get on the computer and search for Viola's identity.

Unfortunately, it appeared that for now this was all we were going to get. When I arrived home to hear the good news, I felt surprised and excited to finally see some documentation on who my grandmother "really" was. The desired information we received was ironic however, as it left us with as many questions as it answered.

Since we could find no information linking my grandmother Viola with her son Edward, it left us to wonder if she gave him up, to be brought up by others? It was also possible that she died at a young age, leaving my dad alone! The questions that filled our minds, are to remain for now, as no history of Viola C. Hewitt can currently be found. Again, time will tell I am sure, as we proceed with our search. The truth will eventually come out, it usually does!

CHAPTER XXV

THE DOWELL GENERATIONS FROM 1683

WILLIAM DOWELL was born in 1683 in Painswick, Gucester, England. He came to the Virginia Colony on a ship called the Hampshire as an indentured servant to John Hancock in 1695 at the age of twelve. He died in 1756 in Dettingen Par, Prince Williams, Virginia. He was the father of Thomas C. Dowell.

THOMAS C DOWELL was born in 1705 in Surry County, Virginia. He died September 6, 1769 in Bedford County, Virginia. He married Elizabeth Sarah in 1727 in Bedford County, Virginia. George Dowell was the first of four sons born to this union.

GEORGE DOWELL was born in 1730 in Prince William County, Virginia and Died in 1772 in Bedford County, Virginia. He married Margaret Ferguson in 1760. They had seven children, one of which was Elijah Dowell their third child.

In May of 1761 on the petition of Thomas C. Dowell, he was exempted from Paying county and public levies for the future, due to old age.

On a deed of gift dated October 7, 1765 from Thomas Dowell to his son George Dowell; .96 acres of land as part of a 196 acre purchase, from a George Byrne. Deed book Q 37.

ELIJAH DOWELL was born about 1765 in Prince William County, Virginia and died August 23, 1821 in Breckenridge County, Kentucky. Elijah Dowell was born on his fathers farm on a branch of Powell's Run near Dumfries, Prince William County, Virginia. Elijah Dowell married Jemima Board on January 15, 1784 in Bedford County, Virginia. They had twelve children, one of which was James Board Dowell born May 15, 1791 in Bedford County, Virginia, their fifth child. Upon Jemima Boards death in 1816, he married Lucy Cain in 1818 in Breckenridge County, Kentucky by William Morris, a Baptist Minister. It is believed that all of Elijah's children were by his first marriage to Jemima Board.

Elijah Dowell was a veteran of the American Revolution and the battle of Guilford Court house north Carolina 1781. According to Lucy's pension application which the United States Government denied possibly because she was his second wife. Elijah was a Private in Captain John Lee's Company, Colonel Parker's Virginia Regiment, it was a 3rd Virginia Regiment of Militia, part of General Edward Stevens small Brigade of 600 men from the frontier counties of Bedford, Rockbridge, Augusta and Botetourt, that stood in the Americans second line at the battle of Guilford Court House.

Elijah and Jemima moved from Bedford County, Virginia probably through the Cumberland Gap, to Hardin (now Breckinridge) County, Kentucky in 1808. He was a farmer at Big Springs, Kentucky.

JAMES BOARD DOWELL was born May 15, 1791 in Bedford County, Virginia. He died on October 20, 1860 in Meade County, Kentucky. He married Barbara Shacklett on February 8, 1812. They had twelve children, one of which was Benjamin Shacklett Dowell, their fifth child. Although Meade County, Kentucky was a peaceful, beautiful place, the area was subjected to two major disasters during James Board's lifetime. On February 21, 1832 the Ohio River reached its banks and was overrun creating the great flood of 1832. It was recorded that houses, and haystacks could be seen floating down the river. This occurred again in 1847 leaving death and destruction throughout Meade County.

The Meade County area also experienced some great times as well, with much growth came large steamships and political gatherings. There were large picnics, races and social get together' s by neighbors living on the farms and small town areas. In stories of that era, it was said that differences between men were usually settled by fisticuffs, rather than shootouts. If a weapon was used by anyone, they were chastised and disgraced, being considered a coward. James Board Dowell was one of the best fist fighters in the county and settled many an argument to his favor, by winning the bout! His character and desire for law and order were unexcelled as he fought for fairness and justice.

BENJAMIN SHACKLETT DOWELL was born on the 30th of November 1818 in Brandenburg, Meade County, Kentucky. He died on November 8, 1880 in El Paso, Texas. He first married Melvina Stith in 1838 and divorced in 1847. His second marriage was to Juana Marquez (a Tigua Indian Princess). They had one daughter and four sons, one of which was Elijah Dowell, the fourth of five children.

Benjamin Shacklett Dowell was also the first Mayor of El Paso, Texas and owned the first saloon there.

ELIJAH DOWELL was born in 1869 in El Paso, Texas. He died on December 15, 1937 in Eddy County, Carlsbad, New Mexico. He married Viloa C. Hewitt on or before 1895 and they had one child, Edward Dowell who was later to become my father.

Elijah Dowell unfortunately fell on bad times after his father's death. He was brought up on an Indian reservation along with his three brothers, as his mother Juana took them there to be near her parents after her husband, Benjamin Shacklett Dowell died. They were not totally accepted and considered half-breeds by the local Indians and sometimes shunned by the white man. This devil may care attitude, left Elijah to seek his own way, knowing little about compassion for others and seeking his enjoyment at the price of anyone who crossed his path.

Elijah Dowell went to prison and left his wife, Viola Hewitt Dowell, pregnant as he was charged with stealing a horse and placed in Huntsville Penitentiary, Texas, ten days before my father Edward Dowell was born. The marriage was short lived, as he never returned to her and she later remarried. When he was ten, he was brought up by a stepfather he never cared much for. Feeling that he had lost his mother to another man, left him anxious and ready to leave home at an early age, which he did.

EDWARD DOWELL was born on July 1, 1895 in Ft. Davis, Texas. He died on June 11, 1979 in Riverside, California. He married Estella Dominguez about 1920. They had twelve children, one of which was Elijah Dowell (James Robert Dowell) born February 9, 1942. Edward Dowell was a hard worker and demanded that from his children also. He spent the first few years of his life working for the railroad and the rest of his life raising a family and working in the fields picking anything that was in season. He was working in the fields until he was in his mid 60's. He also enjoyed raising rabbits and having a small garden in his back yard.

JAMES ROBERT DOWELL was born February 9, 1942 and was named Elijah Dowell but changed his name in 1974 because it never suited him. He worked in the fields until he graduated from high school. He wanted more out of life than to work in the fields, so he went to college as often as he could. His first marriage was to Carole Jackson and they had two children, Eileen Diane Dowell and Eric Gregory Dowell. This marriage did not last and they divorced. In 1979, he met and married Jane Anne Steele Marshall Dowell and they married in June, 1979. James worked for an aerospace corporation, T.R.W. for ten years, getting laid off after working on the project of landing an astronaut on the moon was accomplished. He then went to work for the California Department of Corrections for 25 years and retired and worked an additional five years with the Orange County Probation Department. After retiring there, he went to work at Oak Grove Institution where he presently maintains a part time position working with minor children.

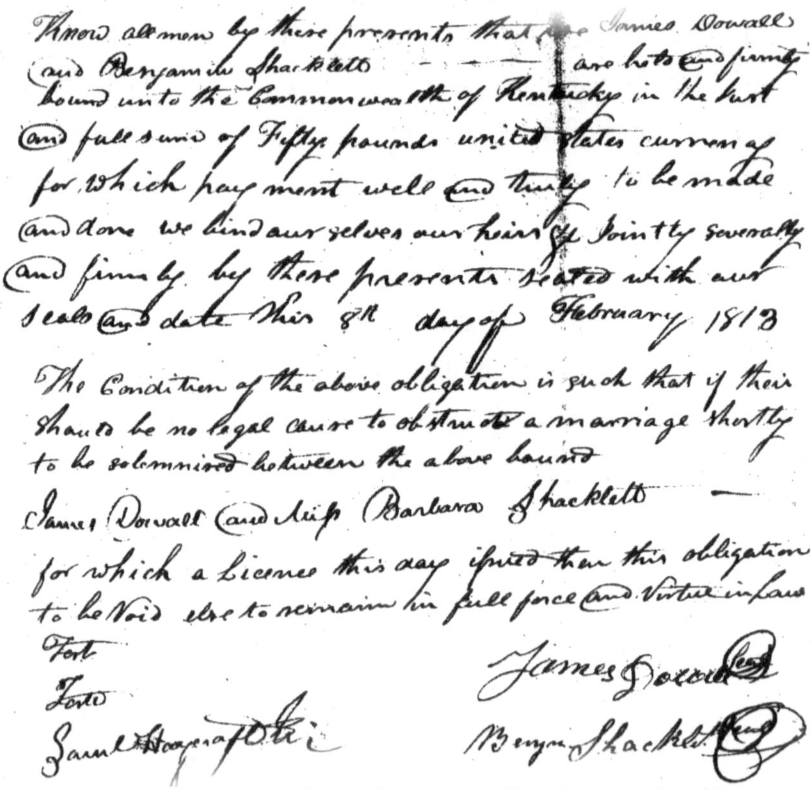

Know all men by these presents that are James Dowall
and Benjamin Shacklett ———— are hold and firmly
bound unto the Commonwealth of Kentucky in the hurt
and full sum of Fifty pounds united states currency
for which payment well and truly to be made
and done we bind our selves our heirs &c Jointly severally
and firmly by these presents seated with our
seals and date this 8th day of February 1813

The Condition of the above obligation is such that if their
should be no legal cause to obstruct a marriage shortly
to be solemnized between the above bound

James Dowall and Miss Barbara Shacklett ——

for which a License this day issued then this obligation
to be Void else to remain in full force and virtue in law
Test
Test
Samuel Hoycraft &c   James Dowall
                                       Benjn Shacklett

Fig. 36   Marriage Agreement: James Board Dowell to Barbara Shacklett
          Date: Feb. 8, 1812   (Actual Signatures)

Appendix

"My Family Tree"
by Meredith Dowell

Thomas Dowell

George Dowell

Elijah Dowell

James Board Dowell

Richard Shacklett Dowell

Elijah Samuel Dowell

Burnis Bryan Dowell

Burnis Meredith Dowell

Burnis Bryan Dowell

Burnis Meredith Dowell

Benjamin Burnis Bryan Dowell

Richard Shacklett Dowell was born in Meade County, Kentucky in 1833. He was the youngest of twelve children born to James B. and Barbara Shacklett Dowell. Richard inherited the family farm and cared for his parents until their deaths. From memory, it seems that Richard initially shared a dual inheritance with his brother, John Aaron Dowell. John ultimately moved his family to Missouri.

By the 1850 census, Richard was 17 years old in his parent's household. His sister, Elizabeth Barnes, had moved back to her parent's home with her young children sometime after the death of her husband in the previous decade. They are also listed in the household in 1850. One may imagine, Richard had the unusual experience of being the "baby" of the family then later relied upon to help out with his younger nieces and nephews.

The James Board Dowell household included slaves. Most of Richard's siblings had inherited their slaves by the time of his formative years. Some domestic slaves were definitely a part of his experience through 1860. I am not sure what crops or livestock the Dowell's worked and so unsure of how much slave labor would have been used in the fields.

I suspect that Richard would have had Confederate sympathies, but have not come across such a record. Like his brother, Ben, his household did not prosper during the war years. The extent of Richard's involvement in the Civil War or his activities during this time are for the most part unknown. He was involved in Freemasonry. The Big Spring Lodge #118 that his brother, Nehemiah, was a member of lists "R.S. Dowell" as a "Past Master" in the years 1864, '65, '69,'70,'71,'73.'74, and 76. Richard had a first cousin in the area with the same initials at this time. Evidence that this R.S. Dowell mentioned in Masonic records was my ggg grandfather is that my Richard has a prominent Masonic emblem on his gravestone and that he is sometimes mentioned as "Mason Dowell" in records.

Richard married his cousin, Mary Elizabeth Hayden in 1855. They had the following Children:

1. Daniel R. Dowell
2. Elijah Samuel "Sam" Dowell
3. Nehemiah "Neam" Burnis Dowell
4. Mary Elizabeth Dowell
5. Roger Hanson "Han" Dowell
6. James Richard Dowell
7. Margaret "Maggie" Dora Dowell

Richard and Mary's first child died in 1857 after only a year of age. Tough start for the young marriage. Mary died in 1881 leaving Richard a widow for the next four years.

Richard married second to Mattie Walker in 1885. Their child:

1. John Stanley Dowell

Census records indicate that Richard and Mattie had two children with only one living.

The First State Bank of Ekron was formed in 1905 with Richard as president.

There were at least three codicils to Richard's Will before his death in 1915. From memory, I think the bulk of his estate was finally left to his wife and son, John.

Richard was 82 years old at the time of his death. His death certificate mentions cancer as a contributing cause.

Only scant oral tradition of Richard survives in my line. A great-granddaughter remembers that he went by "Little Dick" and that his small stature allowed him to serve as a jockey. My grandfather remembered that "Richard was my grandfather's father." He was from Meade County, Kentucky.

I wonder what oral traditions were passed to Richard. His father was a veteran of the war of 1812. His grandfather, a veteran of the Revolution. The family passed through the Cumberland Gap around 1808. The history would have been rich.

More could be drawn out from the record and explored. Would make the reading more interesting. Civil War years, Masonic involvement, widow years--these episodes of Richard's life shaped him in a way that we can only imagine.

Elijah Samuel Dowell
1858-1941

Burnis Bryan Dowell
1895-1932

Burnis Meredith Dowell
1925-

Burnis Bryan Dowell
1951-

Burnis Meredith Dowell
1976-

Benjamin Burnis
Bryan Dowell 2006-

Fig. 32   Burnis (Meredith) Dowell Family Tree

"My Family Tree"
by Tammi and Sharilyn Snyder

Prepared for a U.S. History Class on Dec. 8, 1997

He was half naked as he crossed Texas from Galveston to El Paso, through New Mexico, parts of Arizona and most of Mexico on foot. According to stories handed down from generation to generation, one of my earliest ancestors on my maternal grandmother's side was sired by Alvar Nunez Cabeza de Vaca, the famous Spanish explorer. His written account detailing his adventures from 1525 - 1536, reads like the Arabian Nights, as he and his companions wrested with difficulties, dangers, adversities, savages, and the elements. His name comes from an incident in 1212, when a forefather of Cabeza de Vaca, Martin Alhaja, showed some Spanish kings a secret pathway, by which they might evade mountain passes which were strongly fortified and held by the Moors during the Crusades. The marker Alhaja used was the whitened skull of a cow, which he placed at the entrance to the secret path, so that the kings might enter and surprise their enemies. For this service, he was admitted to the ranks of nobility and his name changed to Cabeza de Vaca, head of a cow.

In 1527, Alvar Nunez Cabeza de Vaca sailed from Spain, around Cuba, and to what's now Tampa Bay, Florida, in America, as second in command of the expedition of Panfilo de Narvaez. After an unsuccessful attempt to conquer Florida, along with a desertion by their ships, the adventurers constructed rafts and headed for Tampico, Mexico. They were shipwrecked on the Texas Coast near Galveston, and in time, death took all but four--Cabeza de Vaca, Castillo, Dorantes, and the black slave Estevan. Cabeza de Vaca's account of the legendary Seven Golden Cities of Cibola inspired the extensive exploration of southern and southwestern North America by Hernando de Soto and Francisco Coronado.

In addition to her direct descendants from Cabeza da Vaca, my maternal grandmother's family was mostly from New Mexico and Mexico. One later Cabeza de Vaca was a governor for the State of New Mexico. However, he served only one day, having died the day after his election. My great, great, great grandfather, Luis Valdez, was an officer in the Mexican Army in Chihuahua. His son, Marcial Valdez, was a New Mexico State Representative, a judge who once tried Billy the Kid, and a businessman who owned the first and only printing press in Las Cruces, New Mexico, before selling it to Wily Lapoint. My maternal grandmother's father, Pedro Pinon, was raised on his family's farm in Las Vegas, New Mexico, and later became a school teacher. He was manager and buyer of Beach's Art Shop in downtown El Paso. The store was stocked with curios from Mexico, Cuba, Japan and China. He traveled extensively to purchase items for the shop.

On my paternal side, the Snyder name was probably changed from the German "Schneider", indicating that the bearer of this name was a tailor. Many German surnames were derived from occupations. My great grandfather, George Alfred Snyder, was born in Fredericksburg, Pennsylvania, in August of 1877, and after spending a short time in Florida as an adult, he moved to Oklahoma. His ancestors included an early governor of Pennsylvania, Simon Snyder, as well as German immigrants, who probably arrived in America between 1600 and 1880. My great grandfather lived in colorful, adventurous times, as he often told of seeing Butch Cassidy and the Sundance Kid, as well as the infamous Dalton brothers.

George Snyder married Effie Valily Simmons (1885-1963) of Irish descent Her father, Squire Adolphus Simmons, was born on Mar 10, 1852, in Perkins County, Georgia, and died in 1943 in Inola, Ok.

Squire Simmons and his family were run out of Georgia for tarring and feathering a carpetbagger. The family regained their place in society in Oklahoma. The Snyder's and Simmon's families were among the first settlers in the Tulsa area, probably as "Sooners" in the Oklahoma Land Rush. Both families helped found Jenks, Ok. And held prominent positions in the town, as well as owning vital businesses, such as the general store, bank, and the livery stable, which evolved into a taxi service after the onset of cars.

George and Effie had ten children, including my grandfather, Kenneth Wilis Snyder (born 1914), who was a Warrant Officer in WWII; Jerry George Snyder, who played professional baseball as shortstop and second baseman for the Washington Senators; and Pauline, whose daughter, Joanne Durant, was a Miss California in the 1950's. Kenneth married Dorothy Esther Dunn (born 1920). Her parents were Elsie Ora Daniels, (born in Lanoma, Iowa around 1887), and James Terrence Dunn (born in Litchfield, Illinois, around 1887). Elsie worked for the telephone company, while James worked at the railroad as a telegraph operator in Pekin, Il. James' surname had been shortened from O'Dunn by a distant relative,. Both of their parents were Irish immigrants who probably arrived in America in the 1840's as a result of the Irish potato famine. The Daniels were of Irish, English and French descent.

My maternal grandfather's family also has a famous person in its history. My great, great grandfather was Benjamin Shacklett Dowell, the first mayor of El Paso. He moved there from Meade County, Kentucky. He was imprisoned in Mexico City in the Mexican-American War, and upon his escape, his knowledge of Spanish helped him get a job supervising Ponce de Leon's vineyards in El Paso, Texas. He married Juana Marquz, a full-blooded Tigua Indian from Ysleta del Sur, and daughter of the tribal Cacique, the head of the tribe. Although the first written history of the Tigua Indians begins with their encounter in New Mexico with Cabeza de Vaca in his journal, oral tradition and archeological evidence push the story back to between 7500 and 12,000 years ago. It is believed that the Tiguas and all Native Americans came from Asia, across a land bridge connecting Siberia and Alaska, and eventually migrated southward to seek new sources of food and strategies for survival. The Anasazi are generally thought to be the ancestors of the Tigua and other modern Pueblo Indians.

Along with many others, Ben Dowell and Juana Marquez Dowell traveled to California in search of gold, but agreed after the birth of their child, Mary, that California was no fit place for a child On the way back to El Paso, while Juana was cooking breakfast, a coyote snuck into the camp and snatched the baby by her clothing, running away with her. At hearing his baby's cry, Dowell picked up his rifle and fired at the coyote, killing it instantly.

Dowell's skills were many, including carpentering, farming, surveying, and butchering. He owned a ranch, the only billiard parlor in town, the first saloon in El Paso, and a grocery store. He was a hotel owner, stage coach stand operator, deputy sheriff, recruiting officer for the Confederate Army, was District Deputy Grand Master of the Masonic Temple, and was El Paso's first postmaster. The Ben Dowell Saloon was the city's gathering place, the town's first official post office, and also served as a court room. Through those doors passed the reserved, the raucous, the rowdy, the lawful, and the awful, the unlawful, the famous and the infamous. Dowell owned a first-class race horse named Kit, who earned him thousands of dollars in bets. Challengers came from Santa Fe, Chihuahua, Missouri, California and Colorado, but Kit never lost a race. Dowell was a fair and innovative mayor, and his daughter, Mary, became one of the first Anglo woman school teachers in El Paso.

Mary Dowell married Warner Phillips, of Scottish and English descent. They had John Newton Phillips, my great grandfather, who married Aurelia Maria Gameros, who bore my grandfather, Robert (Bob) Warner Phillips, born 1911. Bob Phillips was an expert gunsmith, hunter and fisherman, as well as a Captain in WWII. He is 96 years old and living in El Paso. Bob, his sister Aurelia (Chella), his wife Celia Carlota Pinon (born 1910) and my mother, Patricia (Patty) Ann Phillips (born 1951) were all outstanding tennis champions in El Paso, New Mexico, and the entire Southwest. Our family was inducted into the El Paso Tennis Club Hall of Honor, and the Stadium Court (court 1) is dedicated to the Phillips family. My mom met my dad, Terrence Eugene Snyder (born 1946) at UTEP, where both attended school on athletic scholarships -- he for basketball, she for tennis. She married him 25 years ago on Nov 20, 1972. After spending three years in Germany, while my dad served his tour of duty in the Army, they moved to El Paso, where they coached junior high school sports and taught math, science, and physical education. My parents moved to Pearland in 1977, and my dad went into business with his father, Kenneth Willis Snyder. Texas Plumbing Supply, which my grandfather built himself, is still thriving today as our family's business in Houston, Tx. My sister, Sharilyn Annette Snyder (born 1978) and I (born 1981) are both active athletically no doubt due to the athletic prowess of our ancestors. My sister, Shari, continues the championship tradition, as she now attends St. Edward's University in Austin, Tx, on a tennis scholarship.

Though we live in Pearland and have embraced the city as our home, we feel like we have a little sand in our blood from our southwestern roots. El Paso is especially dear to us and we feel as proud as El Paso's mayor, Ray E. Sherman, did when he said these words in the 1930's: "El Paso is a workshop of the new Southwest, the back door of Tx, the front door to Mexico, the side door to NM and AZ, the ground floor of opportunity and the skylight to Heaven -- the last spot kissed by the setting sun on TX soil and the first that will be reached by the return tide of the Pacific Coast immigration. . . El Paso typifies the Land of Tomorrow, the Spirit of Today. We who live there, who have there our hopes and our all, love it for its present, believe in its future and honor its traditions. The courage and labors of an earlier generation have made life there pleasant and sweeter for us today. . . .Born of strong men's hopes, it is the pioneer's dream city come true, a realized vision at the desert's pass a castle in the air that God let stay - the City of the Lily in the Valley of the Rose."

Fig. 33   Robert (Bob) Warner Phillips
          Born August, 1911. Currently Living in El Paso, Texas

THE WANDERER
1536

Alvar Núñez
Cabeza de Vaca

THE annals of exploration hold no more dauntless wanderers than Alvar Núñez Cabeza de Vaca and his three companions, Castillo, Dorantes, and the Moorish slave Estéban. Survivors of the ill-fated Narváez expedition of 1528, they were cast from a raft upon the shores of East Texas in a storm, bereft of their weapons, supplies, even their clothes. Captured naked by Indians and held as slaves, they endured years of captivity before they were able to escape together and set out to find their own people. Clad like savages, these intrepid men walked from the East Coast of Texas hundreds of leagues over desert and mountain to the town of Culiacán near the West Coast of Mexico. First white men to cross the North American continent, their route led them over the Río Grande close by the Pass of the North. With their rude Cross and Christian prayers they were welcomed as healers by friendly tribes who guided and fed them along the way. Eight toilsome years after the wreck of the Narváez expedition, they found their way back to the realm of Spain, bringing the first accounts of the buffalo and the vast, unknown wilderness to the north.

Alvaro Nuñez CABEZA de VACA, and his three companions, Alonso Maldonado, Andrés Dorantes and the Arabian Negro Estevanico, as they passed through the Big Bend country in 1536. That part of the country was, up to 1850 part of El Paso County. For eight years after the disaster of the Narvaez expedition in Florida, he wrested either alone or with his companions with difficulties, dangers, adventures, savages and the elements before arriving safely at Culiacan in Western Mexico.

Fig. 34 Description of Cabeza de Vaca Passing Through El Paso County

The Legend of Ben Dowell

It's been a long time
Since he started his quest
For his place in the sun
And a home in the west.

He rode for long hours
Using rein, spur and rowell.
Ever anxious to settle
Was this man called Ben Dowell.

Sutter's mill and it's gold
Did not suit him, it seems
Instead he kept looking
For the land of his dreams.

Away from the gold fields
But still part of the west
In El Paso, Texas
He put life to test.

Settled down in new Country
With his wife and his Mary
Soon proved to his friends
He could work farm and dairy.

Fig. 35(a) The Legend of Ben Dowell (Page 1 of 4)

The Legend of Ben Dowell
-2-

Ben Dowell's saloon
Was the best place to be
The action was there
Free for all men to see.

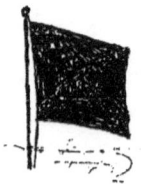

His myriads of friends
Soon learned to acknowledge
That "Uncle" Ben's fairness
Was not learned in College.

When trouble broke out
With the North and the South
Ben took sides with action!!
Not just with his mouth.

The brave way he fought
For a cause — not for glory
Gaining Yankee respect
Is a part of his story.

When peace was secured
For both blue and gray
Ben returned to El Paso
This time to stay.

Fig. 35(b)   The Legend of Ben Dowell   (Page 2 of 4)

The Legend of Ben Dowell
-3-

The town started growing
After Civil war years
And soon it was thriving
In spite of the tears.

FIRST
MAYOR

In the year of our Lord
Eighteen seventy-three
Ben Dowell was mayor
In the land of the free!

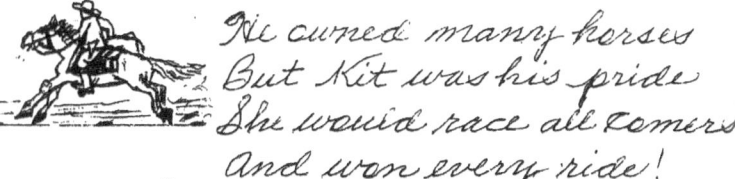

Since water was needed
For life in the west
Ben's law for clean ditches
Was one of his best.

He owned many horses
But Kit was his pride
She would race all comers
And won every ride!

He dreamed of the railroads
For well did he know
That his home in the west
Needed people to grow.

Fig.35(c)   The Legend of Ben Dowell   (Page 3 of 4)

The Legend of Ben Dowell
— 4 —

NOV. 8, 1880

The railroads did come
But too late, for Ben died
Without seeing the day
That would heighten his pride.

The town of El Paso
Has prospered and grown
From seeds of a vision
Ben Dowell had sown.

Celebrating two centuries
Of success unsurpassed
Our Country can thank
Men like Ben Dowell-at long last!

Composed by the inspired pen of
Robert Warner Phillips
Great grandson of
Benjamin Shacklett Dowell
First Mayor of El Paso, Texas.
November 27, 1975.

Illustrated and arrangement by
"Chella" Aurelia M. Phillips

Fig. 35(d)   The Legend of Ben Dowell   (Page 4 of 4)

188

"My Family Tree"
by William John Dowell

JAMES BOARD DOWELL: son of Elijah Dowell and Jemima Board
b. 15 May 1791, Bedford County, Va.
m. 8 Feb 1813, Hardin Co., Ky by Rev. Simeon Buchanan to
    Barbara Shacklett
        b. 26 Apr. 1794, Fayette County, PA Moved to Ky with
           parents in 1796
        D 2 Nov 1873 Meade County, Ky
James and Barbara are both buried in the Dowell family graveyard currently belonging to Richard Bernice "Junior" Dowell, Jr. in Stith Valley near Guston, Meade County, Ky. Tombstone drawing by Lucille Seymour shows Barbara's date of death as 2 Nov. 1874 (not 1873)

NANCY DOWELL (SISTER OF Benjamin Shacklett Dowell, first mayor of El Paso)
b. 15 Jan 1817, Meade County, Ky
m. 8 Oct. 1835 Meade County, Ky to her first cousin, William
    Harrison Dowell.
d. 9 Apr 1905, Meade County, Ky
        WILLIAM HARRISON DOWELL, son of George Dowell
        and Mary "Polly" Ann
        Wimp. George was the elder brother of James Board
        Dowell. Polly was the daughter of John Wimp and Roxina
        Kirkpatrick.
        b. 11 May 1816, Big Aprings, Hardin (now Breckinridge)
          County, Ky
        d. 21 Aug 1892, Meade Co., Ky
        Both buried in Dowell Family Cemetery, Stith Valley, Meade
        Co., Ky

SIMEON HORACE DOWELL

b. 30 Apr 1843, Meade Co., Ky

m. 6 Oct 1864, Meade Co., Ky at the Mary Elizabeth Walker Hayden farmhouse by Rev. George H. Hicks, Baptist minister to Rebecca Jane Hayden.
Moved to Missouri in 1877.

d. 27 May 1932, Brookfield, Linn County, Mo
Rebecca Jane Hayden was the daughter of Daniel Fulton Hayden and Mary Elizabeth Walker.
b. 18 Feb. 1847, Meade Co., Ky
d. 6 Oct 1889 in Missouri, died on a trip while visiting relatives, buried Mt. Zion Cemetery, Edgerton, Platte County, Mo.

WILLIAM HORACE DOWELL

b. 11 Feb. 1888, Mike, Cariton County, Mo

m. 3 Aug. 1909, Brookfield, Linn County, Mo by Rev. A. L. Zink to Alpha Mayme Green.

d. 8 Mar. 1976, Salisbury, Chariton County, Mo
Alpha Mayme Green was the daughter of Thomas Stout Green and Martha Jane Paxton
b. 12 Feb 1890, Westville, Chariton County, Mo
d. 12 Nov 1972, Salisbury, Chariton County, Mo.

Both buried Salisbury City Cemetery, Mo.

EARL SIMEON DOWELL

b. 18 Jan. 1912, Parsons, Labette Count, Ks

m/2 on 31 Aug 1940 at Palmyra, Marion County, Mo. To Margaret Lois Hatch

d. 3 Aug, 2001, Fairfax Hospital, Fairfax County, Va.

Buried Arlington National Cemetery

Margaret Lois Hatch is the daughter of John Franklin Hatch and Bessie Maude Powell.

B. 30 July 1915 in a farmhouse in Whiteflock, Mc Donough County, Il.

WILLIAM JOHN DOWELL

b. 1944, Washington, D.C.

m/2 in 1989, Milton Keynes, England to Irene Carol Anne Stamford.

William and Irene have 1 daughter, Emma Jane

"MY FAMILY TREE"
BY MARK DOWELL

My great, great grandfather was GEORGE DOWELL, born 11-24-1788, Bedford County, Va. His parents-Elijah and Jemima Board Dowell. George was their 4th child and the brother of James Board Dowell (child #5). George moved to Breckenridge County, Ky in 1808 with his parents and on 9-6-1813 married my great, great grandmother, Mary Ann Wimp. (She is the daughter of John Wimp and Roxina Kirkpatrick and they both came from Ireland.)

George and Mary had 12 children which the 12th child, Benjamin M. Dowell was my great grandfather. He was born 4-17-1837 in Hardin County, Ky. George passed on 3-30-1842 and Mary passed on 12-16-1877 and are both buried about 2 miles outside of Big Springs on land George owned.

BENJAMIN M. DOWELL married Nancy Spires on 5-21-1808. She died very young and is buried next to George and Mary Dowell. On 3-4-1874, Benjamin married my great grandmother, Mary Jane Abell. According to the 1880 census, Benjamin was deaf. He was one of the Dowell's that stayed in Big Springs while many of his brothers and sisters moved west.

On 6-5-1879 my grandfather WILLIE PATE DOWELL was born. He was the 3rd of 4 children born to Benjamin and Mary Dowell. His 2 oldest brothers moved West and his youngest brother moved to Meade County, Ky. This left my grandfather the only Dowell family left in Big Springs from George and Mary Dowell. Willie Pate married Nettie Miller, my grandmother on 8-26-1903 in Hardin County. Willie Pate was a farmer in Big Springs as was his father and grandfather. The 4th child of Willie Pate and Nettie was my father, WILLIE ADRON DOWELL born 8-12-1916. Nettie passed away two weeks after giving birth to their 5th child, Edith Dowell. The date of her death was 4-2-1918. Willie Pate married again on 7-30-1919 to Lillie Carter. My father was 2 years old when his mother died and said Lillie was a very good mother. Willie Pate passed on 4-20-1933 and Lillie passed in 1967 and both are buried at the Big Springs Baptist Church as is Benjamin and Mary Dowell. My father married Ernestine Farrow and they moved to Louisville, Ky. Edith was the only Dowell that stayed in Big Springs with her family. Her daughter, Brenda still lives there.

I, Mark Dowell, was born in 1957 in Louisville, Ky and continue to live here. I have one sister, Sherry, who lives in New Albany, Indiana. I am married and have 3 children and 2 grandchildren.

I have enjoyed doing the Dowell Family history and meeting so many cousins which I would never have known about if I didn't do this. There is so much history in the Dowell Family and I am so proud to be a part of it.

"My Family Tree"
by Richard Bernice Dowell

WILLIAM HARRISON DOWELL (1816-1892) Married Nancy Dowell (1817-1905)

> They had 12 children. Number 3 was:

JAMES HARRISON DOWELL (1841-1913) Married Mary Ann Blissett (1850-1873)

> They had 5 children. Number 4 was:

ELIJAH MELVIL DOWELL (1868-1924) Married Dora R. (Becky) Allen

> They had 10 children. Number 2 was:

RICHARD BERNICE DOWELL (1894-1983 Married Hattie (N)

> They had 7 children. Number 5 was:

RICHARD BERNICE DOWELL JR Married Anna Frances Snelling

Elijah Dowell (b 1765) and Jemima Board Dowell b 1766)

12 Children:

Elizabeth Dowell	Born abt. 1784
Nancy Dowell	Born abt. 1785
Nehemiah Dowell	Born abt. 1785
George Dowell	Born abt. 1788
James Board Dowell	Born abt. 1791
John Dowell	Born abt. 1793
Elijah Dowell Jr.	Born abt. 1800
Jane "Jincer" Dowell	Born abt. 1803
Joel Dowell	Born abt. 1805
Mary Polly Dowell	Born abt. 1806
Harrison Dowell	Born abt .1807
Dandridge Dowell	Born abt. 1809

James Board Dowell (b abt. 1791) and Barbara Shacklett (b abt. 1794)

12 children:

Nancy Dowell	Born abt. 1812
Elizabeth Dowell	Born abt. 1814
Jemima Dowell	Born abt. 1815
Elijah R. Dowell	Born abt. 1817
Benjamin Shacklett. Dowell	Born abt. 1818
John Aaron Dowell	Born abt. 1821
Nehemiah D. Dowell	Born abt. 1827
Sarah K. Dowell	Born abt. 1823
James M. Dowell	Born abt. 1825
Mary S. Dowell	Born abt. 1826
Susannah Jane Dowell	Born abt. 1830
Richard Shacklett Dowell	Born abt. 1833

Benjamin Shacklett Dowell (b. abt. 1818) and Juana Marquez (b abt. 1839)

5 Children:

Mary Marquez Dowell	Born abt. 1854
John R. Dowell (Juan)	Born abt. 1862
Nehemiah Dowell (Nim)	Born abt. 1866
Elijah Dowell (Lige)	Born abt. 1869
Richard Dowell	Born abt. 1875

El Paso 100 Year Centennial

Fig. 37   El Paso Street around 1873

"SOUTH EL PASO STREET"

This drawing depicted what El Paso looked like, looking down South
El Paso Street on May 17, 1873, the date of the city's incorporation.
The drawing adorned placemats that were used to celebrate a dinner
in honor of the 100th anniversary of the City of El Paso.

Following incorporation, the first City Council meeting took place in
Ben Dowell's saloon on August 15, 1873. El Paso at the time was a
small mud thatched village on the banks of the Rio Grande, and its
main street was South El Paso Street.

On July 17, 1973, the City of El Paso paid tribute to the strong men
and women who explored and pioneered the West and who founded
El Paso.

Sources and References

Mary Dowell Phillips Memoirs

Unpublished interview of Mary Dowell Phillips regarding early days in El Paso, Texas, by Major Richard F. Burges on May 26, 1934.

El Paso City Library, newspapers and literature

El Paso Herald Post, newspapers, literature

El Paso Daily Herold

El Paso Times

Louisville City Library

Nancy Hamilton's "Ben Dowell, El Paso's First Mayor" 1976

C. L. Sonnichsen's "Pass of the North" 1968

C. L. Sonnichsen's "The El Paso Salt War of 1877"

W. W. Mills, "Fourty Years at El Paso, 1858-1898" (Rex W. Strickland)

Military records of Benjamin S. Dowell, National Archives, Washington, D.C.

Records of El Paso County, Texas. Deed Book A 83

El Paso County Deed Records Book "F" 85-E, pg 8l, F-pg 286, 211. Book C.P. 590 Book E-34, Book J. Pg 49, Book E pp 163-164 Book F pg 397 Book B Pp 501-502

Interviews, letters, records, newspaper reports and books from family members in El Paso; Robert (Bob) Phillips, Texas- grandson of Mary Dowell Phillips.(Great Grandson to Benjamin S. Dowell)

Patricia Snyder of Texas, daughter of Robert Phillips and Great granddaughter of Mary Dowell Phillips. (great, great granddaughter to Benjamin S. Dowell)

Mary Jane Edwards of Texas, daughter of Robert Phillips and Great granddaughter of Mary Dowell Phillips. (great, great granddaughter to Benjamin S. Dowell)

Meredith Dowell, Tennessee.- Great, great grandson of Richard Shacklett Dowell, (brother of Benjamin Shacklett Dowell) (Son of Elijah and Jemima Board Dowell)

William J. (Bill) Dowell of Va.-Great, great grandson of Nancy Dowell, (sister of Benjamin Shacklett Dowell) and William Harrison Dowell (son of Elijah and Jemima Board Dowell.

Mark Dowell of Kentucky.- Great, great grandson of George Dowell, (brother of James Board Dowell) (son of Elijah and Jemima Board Dowell)

Richard Bernice (Junior) and Anna Francis Dowell, Kentucky

Louise Havens of Kansas from the family of Dowell's through Elijah Richard. (brother of Benjamin Shacklett Dowell) and son of James Board Dowell.

Peggy Glover, great, great granddaughter of Nehemiah Dowell. (son of Benjamin Shacklett Dowell)

About the Author

A desire at a young age to write and understand human behavior, brought James to seek a major in Behavorial Science and a minor in English Literature.

He began his professional career in 1962 with T.R.W. Systems, an aerospace corporation. This involved processing data on various missile firings at Cape Canaveral, Florida, and preparing reports for engineers. His tenure of eight years ended with the landing of astronauts on the moon in 1969. His layoff due to government cutbacks, resulted in his seeking and obtaining employment with the California Department of Corrections in 1972. His assignment to death row, where the notorious Charlie Manson followers were housed, as well as an assignment to the psychiatric ward, gave him the opportunity to utilize his writing skills. This included incident and disciplinary reports, as well as directives, policies and procedures. Upon retiring after twenty five years of service, he had reached the level of Supervising Counselor.

James is currently employed at a private institution for mentally challenged minors.

His continued desire to express himself through his literary talents, has resulted in many short stories and this, his second book. He truly feels that his desire and ease of expression is a gift from above, that he deeply appreciates.

www.ingramcontent.com/pod-product-compliance
Lightning Source LLC
Chambersburg PA
CBHW061401280526
45784CB00001B/334